Critical Guides to French Texts

71 Verlaine: Fêtes galantes *and* Romances sans paroles

Critical Guides to French Texts

EDITED BY ROGER LITTLE, WOLFGANG VAN EMDEN,
DAVID WILLIAMS

VERLAINE

Fêtes galantes *and*
Romances sans paroles

Susan Taylor-Horrex

Lecturer in French Studies
University of Lancaster

Grant & Cutler Ltd
1 9 8 8

© Grant & Cutler Ltd
1988

ISBN 0-7293-0290-3

I.S.B.N. 84-599-2547-1

DEPÓSITO LEGAL: v. 2.676-1988

Printed in Spain by
Artes Gráficas Soler, S. A., Valencia
for

GRANT & CUTLER LTD
55-57 GREAT MARLBOROUGH STREET, LONDON W1V 2AY

For Emily and Stella

Acknowledgements

M Y grateful thanks are due to Professor Roger Little for his courteous assistance and encouragement; to Dr Keith Wren, who read the manuscript and made many valuable comments and suggestions; to Anthony Heward for his comments on Debussy's and Fauré's settings of the poems; to Mrs Anne Dalton, who thoughtfully and efficiently typed the manuscript; and to many French Studies students whose enthusiasm for Verlaine has always been a source of encouragement and insight.

Contents

Contents

Prefatory Note

As references to the poems are by their titles, any good edition may be used. For present purposes, I recommend the Garnier Flammarion edition (*7*) because it contains Verlaine's writings on Rimbaud and consequently fills out much of the biographical matter. For all quotations from Verlaine other than the poems, reference is made to the latest Pléiade edition (*1*). Italicised numbers in parentheses, followed, if appropriate, by a page number, refer to items in the selective bibliography at the end of the volume.

Introduction

FÊTES galantes and *Romances sans paroles* are, respectively, the second and fourth collections of Verlaine's poetry. Published in 1869 and 1874, they are the work of a relatively young man. It is my view, and the argument of this book, that *Fêtes galantes* and *Romances sans paroles* contain the best of Verlaine's distinctive art, an art I term symbolist impressionism, by which I understand a poetry evoking near-disembodied sensuous impressions which symbolise the poet's emotional state. Impressionism, usually applied to a movement in painting, denotes an art of the fleeting moment, of the outward gaze. Apparently unstructured, its transitory images and casual composition deal mainly with the effects of light and weather, especially on landscape. Symbolism, a literary as well as pictorial movement, deals, on the other hand, with the inward gaze. It is concerned with individual sensations, impressions, intuitions, with dreams and myths. Verlaine's poetic art combines elements of these two movements. His poetic symbolism is that of ephemeral and ever shifting sensations as distinct from the more solid and static sensations of other symbolist writers. Together the collections chart Verlaine's development of this art which reaches its perfection in some of the *Romances sans paroles*. This art of symbolist impressionism, which can be regarded as a specifically musical poetry, is already evident in his first collection, *Poèmes saturniens* (1866), in particular, the 'Paysages tristes'. Indeed in a letter of 22 November accompanying a copy of the poems which Verlaine sent to the poet, Stéphane Mallarmé, he refers to 'un effort vers l'Expression, vers la Sensation rendue' (*4*, vol. I, p. 929), a poetry primarily concerned with the expression of the individual experience and sensibility.

Verlaine was born in 1844. A long-awaited child, he was greatly and permanently indulged by his mother. His life is a pattern of seeking escape from his own self-destructiveness. His undemanding employment in the Hôtel de Ville in Paris left him free to pursue his true interest, poetry. His first collection, *Poèmes saturniens,* was published when he was twenty-two. The death in the following year of his elder cousin, Elisa Dujardin, who had paid for the poems to be published, and who, just as importantly, appears to have given Verlaine some kind of moral directive, reactivated Verlaine's bouts of drinking, characterised by extreme violence. The escape in drink from pain and responsibility was illusory. In 1869, the year in which the *Fêtes galantes* were published, Verlaine met Mathilde Mauté de Fleurville who, at sixteen, was some nine years younger than he was. Their engagement in October of that year was followed by marriage in the year after.

Verlaine's early apprenticeship with the Parnassian poets was vital to the formation of his distinctive poetic art. This group of poets, named after the occasional review, *Le Parnasse contemporain,* which published their poems between March and July 1866, and of which Leconte de Lisle was the acknowledged leader, held the artistic ideal of restoring purity to a poetry which had degenerated as a result of the excessive emotional effusion of Romantic poetry (as most clearly typified in the verse of Alfred de Musset). The Parnassians aspired to a formal perfection comparable to that of sculpture, as Gautier makes clear in his poem-manifesto 'L'Art' (*L'Artiste,* 1857):

> Oui, l'œuvre sort plus belle
> D'une forme au travail
>   Rebelle,
> Vers, marbre, onyx, émail.   (1-4)

Already in 1834, in his preface to his novel, *Mademoiselle de Maupin,* Gautier is proposing an art for art's sake, which he defines in the review *L'Artiste* of 14 December as 'un travail dégagé de toute préoccupation autre que celui du beau en lui-même'. Parnassian poetry then was not simply a question of impeccable poetic technique. It was to be a poetry free not only from too much emotionalism, but also from the social, religious and political moralising for which the Parnassians criticised Victor Hugo's *La Légende des siècles* (1859). It aimed then to purify poetry. It was an impersonal poetry, which is not the same as an impassive poetry, a characteristic sometimes and mistakenly attributed to Parnassianism. An objective, some would say eternal, truth about the human condition is expressed, usually through a precisely drawn scene. The extent of the picture's formal perfection is itself a comment on the purity and truth of what it expresses; formal beauty is simultaneously the beauty of an objective truth. De Lisle's portrait of the jaguar in 'Le rêve du jaguar', from his *Poèmes barbares* (1862) 'tells' of the delicate tension between peace and violence, harmony and discord.

Verlaine's progress toward a poetry of near-disembodied sensations and emotions clearly derives from his early involvement with the Parnassian poets and undoubtedly from the musicians associated with the Parnassians, such as Chabrier, whom Verlaine met at the bookshop of Alphonse Lemerre, publisher to the Parnassians.

Yet other influences are equally evident in the collections, in particular the intimate lyrical poetry of Lamartine and, especially, of Marceline Desbordes-Valmore. Verlaine's response to Desbordes-Valmore's poetry, 'la passion bien exprimée' (2, p. 671) with its delicate emotional tones, is evident in *Fêtes galantes* and *Romances sans paroles*. The poems obviously benefit too from the influence of Baudelaire. His collection of poems *Les Fleurs du mal* (1857) gave the example of the poet as craftsman striving to realise the music inherent in poetry, a coherent arrangement of reciprocal relationships both formal and semantic. This is based on the poet's apprehension of a system of 'correspondances' or links in the external world. The perception of these links, by analogy, is experienced through the senses. The technical mastery and the expression of subtly varied sensations in the collections owe much to *Les Fleurs du mal,* without in any way being uninspired imitations of them. Where Baudelaire and Verlaine differ significantly is in the moral dimension of their work. Baudelaire writes of the individual as a physical as well as a moral and spiritual being. Verlaine confines himself to the sensuous and emotional individual. This is the core of the poems' 'argument', if 'argument' there be; and so of their always highly suggestive ambiguity.

But the catalyst for Verlaine's perfected art in *Romances sans paroles* is the influence of Arthur Rimbaud. It is an art towards which the poetry of *Fêtes galantes* is already moving. It is plausible to speculate whether Verlaine's poetry would have achieved the degree of mastery it did without the influence of Rimbaud. Certainly it would not have gone so far in the direction of evocation of sensation and mood, and might have developed in a different direction altogether, towards more beautiful refined verbal pictures along the lines of *Fêtes galantes,* for instance, but carrying little suggestive significance. Given the extremes of Verlaine's emotional moods, it seems likely that a catalyst less dramatic than Rimbaud's personality, his art and Verlaine's relationship with him would not have been particularly powerful. I am wary of considering biography in conjunction with the art produced out of that life, believing that Verlaine's poetry, like any other artist's work of quality, can and does 'mean' something in its own right. Nonetheless *Romance sans paroles* derive so manifestly from Verlaine's and Rimbaud's relationship and, as likely or not, would not have been written otherwise, that I consider some brief biographical details to be a useful illumination of the poems and especially of the way in which Rimbaud was a catalyst for what was already Verlaine's unique and distinctive poetic art. It must however be stressed that the biographical details are in no way an *explanation* of the poems.

Rimbaud had sent letters and poems (September 1871) to Verlaine, who responded with a summons to Paris: 'Venez chère grande âme, on vous appelle, on vous attend' (*4,* vol. I, p. 967). The young poet arrived on 10 September 1871, at a critical moment. By this time, Verlaine's marriage to Mathilde, then eight months pregnant, was already in trouble. Verlaine was ready for someone new, for a new way of life.

That this new person was a young adolescent male catalysed Verlaine's repressed and guilt-ridden homosexuality, which of course made his passion all the stronger. Love, sex, a bohemian way of life, these were all embodied for Verlaine in the person of Rimbaud. So too was renewed artistic creation. Verlaine had written little or no poetry during his marriage to Mathilde. Indeed his last collection of poems, *La Bonne Chanson* (published before their marriage), had mainly been composed of trite and derivative poems about the salvation and happiness he hoped for from marriage.

Rimbaud initially stayed with the Verlaines; it was a short-lived stay, for his unsociable manner and physical self-neglect quickly made him unacceptable. Thereafter he led a peripatetic existence among Verlaine's friends in Paris. Verlaine all but left the marital home too; he and Rimbaud spent much time together, drinking and probably sleeping together and generally scandalising the artistic circles in which, at least to begin with, Rimbaud had been greeted as a genius. Their life together was interrupted by the birth of Verlaine's son Georges on 30 October 1871, but Verlaine's return home was short-lived: he left Mathilde again for Rimbaud in January 1872 after an extremely violent scene, during which he threw their baby son against the wall and tried to strangle his wife. For the next eighteen months, Verlaine and Rimbaud lived together. The pain suffered by both was considerable. Verlaine was besotted by the youthful poet, who often treated him cruelly. Mallarmé understood much of the lasting and devastating effect Rimbaud had on Verlaine when he referred to Rimbaud as 'ce passant considérable' (*24*, p. 512). Rimbaud was the significant person and love in Verlaine's life. Rimbaud for his part was undoubtedly burdened by the weak, self-indulgent and chronically irresponsible Verlaine, who, moreover, appeared not to understand what Rimbaud was seeking to achieve in poetry. The relationship was spent mainly in three places, Paris, Belgium and London. The 'Paysages belges' and 'Aquarelles' clearly derive from these travels; the 'Ariettes' reflect the more intimate side of the relationship. In July 1872 Verlaine and Rimbaud left for Belgium. Mathilde, seeking a reconciliation, met

Verlaine at the Hôtel Liégeois in Brussels on 22 July and persuaded him to return with her. Verlaine boarded the train with her, only to jump off at the frontier. Mathilde then demanded a separation and put the matter in the hands of a solicitor. This legal formality was to trouble Verlaine a great deal in its decisiveness. Verlaine and Rimbaud spent six weeks travelling around Belgium, often on foot. In September, they went to London. Verlaine's chronic dependency is revealed in an incident of late 1872. Rimbaud returned home to Charleville in November. Verlaine fell ill and convinced his mother he was dying. Indulgent as ever, Mme Verlaine travelled to London, and, at Verlaine's demand, sent for Rimbaud and paid his fare! At the beginning of April 1873, Verlaine and Rimbaud returned to Brussels, Rimbaud leaving shortly afterwards for Charleville where he worked on *Une Saison en enfer,* his repudiation of his innovative poetry and, in some respects, of his relationship with Verlaine (see 'Alchimie du verbe'). Verlaine meantime went to stay with an aunt and to worry about the impending lawsuit Mathilde was bringing against him. The poets were back in London together by the end of May, their relationship under heavy financial and emotional strain. Matters became so bad that in July 1873 Verlaine left, for Brussels, to seek a reconciliation with Mathilde. Once more at the Hôtel Liégeois, he wrote to Mathilde, Rimbaud and his mother, threatening to commit suicide if Mathilde did not return to him. In the event it was Verlaine's mother who went to Brussels, where she was joined by Rimbaud on 8 July. Rimbaud found the situation intolerable and decided to leave for Paris, whereupon Verlaine threw a tantrum and fired a shot which happened to catch Rimbaud's wrist. Outside the hotel, Verlaine once more restrained Rimbaud who, understandably fearing for his life, sought help from a policeman. Verlaine was arrested and subsequently sentenced to two years' imprisonment.

The poems of *Romances sans paroles* were written during, after, and as a consequence of this intense two-year period in Verlaine's life. 'Poésie pure' many of the poems certainly are, but they nonetheless offer an aesthetic autobiography, for there can be no doubt that Rimbaud and Verlaine influenced each other's aesthetic ideas ... after all, for both of them this was arguably the most poetically innovative period of their respective careers. Of relevance here is Rimbaud's ideal of a 'poésie objective', a poetry perceived by an impersonal self ('JE est un autre, *35*, p. 249), purified of conventional responses and so able to perceive a pure, uncontaminated world. Rimbaud terms this perception 'voyance', the fresh world seen, 'vu'. This impersonal self echoes, albeit in a new way, Verlaine's early Parnassianism and can be equated with Verlaine's removal, in *Fêtes galantes,* of the thinking self in favour of the feeling self (see below, pp. 28-29). Rimbaud's poetic world of the 'vu' is that of the senses. So too is Verlaine's, but it is of a different order; Verlaine's senses remain firmly located in himself, not in the world of the 'vu' as is the case with Rimbaud, for instance in the latter's poem 'Le bateau ivre'. From the aesthetic point of view, then, Rimbaud did not so much influence Verlaine as be the right kind of catalyst at the right time for developing what is essentially Verlaine's own art of near-disembodied sensations. Rimbaud had, after all, designated Verlaine as the second God, a 'voyant' after Baudelaire, in his letter of 15 May 1871 to Paul Demeny: 'la nouvelle école, dite parnassienne, a deux voyants, Albert Mérat et Paul Verlaine, un vrai poète' (*35*, p. 254). And Verlaine's reference to his 'Dédicace' of *Romances sans paroles* to Rimbaud (ultimately withdrawn on the advice of his friend and publisher, Lepelletier) confirms this in its more pragmatic aspects:

> Je tiens beaucoup à la dédicace à Rimbaud. D'abord comme protestation, puis parce que ces vers ont été faits, lui étant là et m'ayant poussé beaucoup à les faire. (*8,* vol. I, pp. 101-02)

Verlaine's return to Catholicism in Mons prison in June 1874 repeated the pattern of seeking refuge from his self-destructiveness. He spent the next four years teaching French in various schools in England, 'fathering' his pupil, Lucien Létinois, whom he had taught while teaching at Notre-Dame de Rethel in late 1877, and with whom he improbably set up a farming enterprise in 1880 which, less improbably, failed.

With Létinois's early death in 1883, and doubtless some time before that, there began the long and sad decline from a degree of emotional and artistic well-being, a decline regularly punctuated by violent episodes (for example he spent a month in prison in 1885 for attempting to strangle his mother). His final years from 1886 to 1896 were those of the seedy drunken bohemian, his lodgings alternating between wretched hotel rooms and hospitals, in particular the Hôpital Broussais, where medical care was backed up by amazingly understanding doctors who allowed Verlaine to hold what were effectively literary salons from his hospital bed. The home help, as it were, came from two women, Philomène Boudin and Eugénie Krantz, between whom Verlaine shared his affections and afflictions before eventually settling down with Eugénie, who was with him when he died on 8 January 1896.

Verlaine's imprisonment and subsequent absence from France certainly contributed to the fact that his work was virtually unknown in that country for some ten years, whereas he himself was known by his reputation for being a terrible and evil 'pervert'. Yet from 1882 he became very much a legend in his own lifetime. On 10 November of that year *Paris-moderne* published his poem 'L'Art poétique' (later part of the collection *Jadis et naguère,* 1885), which drew the attention of a young poet, Charles Morice. Morice introduced Verlaine's work to other poets of the younger generation, among them Stuart Merrill, Francis Vielé-Griffin and Henri de Régnier, who effectively became his disciples. J.-K. Huysmans consecrated both Verlaine and his poetry in his novel *A rebours,* in which the 'hero' Des Esseintes's purpose in life is to create an aesthetic existence in reaction against contemporary materialism, one of his methods being to read the *Poèmes saturniens.* Verlaine's reputation principally rests upon this collection together with *Fêtes galantes, Romances sans paroles* and, interestingly, on *Les Poètes maudits* (1884, 2, pp. 635-91). This collection of essays introduced French readers to poets either unknown, such as Rimbaud, or unfairly passed over, for instance Marceline Desbordes-Valmore. So the poetry upon which his reputation is justly based was already written by the time he had acquired his following of younger poets and was writing qualitatively inferior poetry, matched by a life of equally distressing poverty and generally outrageous dependency.

1

Impossible Lands: Themes in *Fêtes galantes*

IN essence, Verlaine's poems treat the theme of the divided self: in *Fêtes galantes* the passive versus the active self, in *Romances sans paroles* the irresponsible versus the responsible self. As such, *Fêtes galantes* and *Romances sans paroles* take a different approach from *La Bonne Chanson* and *Sagesse* which treat the theme of the weak self to be saved, respectively, by marriage to Mathilde and returning to God, and where the conflict is somewhat externalised. With *Fêtes galantes* and *Romances sans paroles* the conflict remains firmly located within the poet's self.

Not surprisingly then, in comparison with these other collections, *Fêtes galantes* and *Romances sans paroles* have a predominantly emotional rather than intellectual content. To illustrate my point, I will take two examples. The first is from *Romances sans paroles*:

> Il pleure dans mon cœur
> Comme il pleut sur la ville;
> Quelle est cette langueur
> Qui pénètre mon cœur?
> ('Ariettes oubliées', III, 1-4)

The second is from *La Bonne Chanson*:

> Je veux, guidé par vous, beaux yeux aux flammes douces,
> Par toi conduit, ô main où tremblera ma main,
> Marcher droit, que ce soit par des sentiers de mousses
> Ou que rocs et cailloux encombrent le chemin;
> (IV, 17-20)

Obviously the themes of both quotations concern the emotions; the difference is in the *way* the theme is treated. The first example evokes an emotional state of mind, the second presents a more intellectualised emotional attitude, here, in the form of Verlaine's hopes for the future. It is precisely this difference between the *evoked* and the *reasoned* states of emotion which distinguishes Verlaine's original art of *Fêtes galantes* and *Romances sans paroles,* the art of symbolist impressionism. In these collections the emotional states of mind *are* the themes.

Fêtes galantes and *Romances sans paroles* deal with the theme of the divided self specifically in the area of love. In an important respect all the poems in the collections treat love. It is the central theme. Some poems present a related theme but this always refers back, directly or indirectly, to the dominant theme of love. The thematic pattern of both collections is, then, multidimensional as distinct from exclusively linear and progressive.

This is not to say that the thematic presentation is static, a random assortment of emotional moods. Both collections present a range of shifting emotional nuances, and both collections are shaped by an evolution in the nature of Verlaine's conflict with himself and consequently in his way of loving. The development from passive versus active self to a clearer confrontation of the irresponsible with the responsible self (already hinted at in *Fêtes galantes*) will equally be the argument of my discussion of the themes of *Fêtes galantes* and *Romances sans paroles.* Change is rarely satisfyingly straightforward. We often come full circle before we are able to move forward. And change does not necessarily mean improvement. This is perhaps the deepest exemplification of Verlaine's *other* 'art poétique', 'L'art, mes enfants, c'est d'être absolument soi-même' (*Bonheur,* XVIII, 35). In the light of this contention, I propose therefore to discuss the themes of *Fêtes galantes* and *Romances sans paroles* in separate chapters.

In *Fêtes galantes* there are three distinct aspects; echoes of the paintings of Watteau and of the poetry of Hugo, and the themes of love and passivity. I shall consider these aspects as

three 'layers' in the poems and show that, in a small number
of poems, these three layers merge so as to be indistinguish-
able. This kind of merging, I believe, is the hallmark of
Verlaine's distinctive poetry, a form of pure poetry, which
creates its own world and terms of reference and is the vital
link with Verlaine's poetic art of the finest poems of *Romances sans paroles*.

In one important respect the title of *Fêtes galantes* is its
theme, for it denotes the complex nature of the detached
perspective on love, that least detached of emotions. Verlaine's
title is commonly attributed to the influence of Watteau's
eighteenth-century genre of painting of the same name, and
to Victor Hugo's poem, 'La Fête chez Thérèse' (*Les Contemplations,* I, 22, 1840, published 1856). Watteau (1684-1721)
is credited with having developed the genre of the *fête
galante*. Broadly speaking, by the beginning of the eighteenth
century, the *fête galante* was an idealised country scene
peopled by aristocratic figures, originally the new élite of the
city which, under the Regency, and in rivalry with the court
after the death of Louis XIV, went to the 'country' (in reality
the Paris suburbs) to 'commune with nature'. The *fête galante* soon became a fashionable feature of much literature
and opera of the period and, by the time of Watteau, it
'représente une adaptation *moderne,* désacralisée et peut-être
nostalgique d'un art de Cour en voie de disparition' (*39,*
p. 496). Some of Watteau's paintings depict a landscaped
nature with beautifully dressed people who are freed from the
constraints of daily life to indulge in amorous pursuits in a
timeless world of music and dance (*La Perspective, Les Plaisirs du bal*); 'Their occupation is pleasure'.[1] Other paintings
show *commedia dell'arte* characters either singly (*Pierrot dit
autrefois Gilles*) or in groups (*L'Amour au théâtre italien*).
Many depict musicians (*L'Enchanteur*). Occasionally aristocratic figures and *commedia* characters are depicted together

---

[1] W. G. Kalnein and M. Levey, *Art and Architecture of the Eighteenth
Century in France,* Pelican History of Art (London, Penguin, 1972), p. 18.

(*Les Plaisirs du bal, Pierrot content*), but then the *commedia* character is usually Pierrot, the tragic clown, often associated with Watteau himself:

> Il y a ... dans l'œuvre, un évident sentiment d'auto-identification qui nous concerne comme elle concerne le peintre. Coupé du monde qui l'entoure, sans un mouvement, isolé et seul, *Pierrot,* image poignante et gauche, reste unique dans l'histoire de l'art. (*39*, p. 434)

Certainly the way the Pierrot figure gazes at and beyond the assembled group in *Les Plaisirs du bal* and out to the spectator conveys a detached, ironical approach to the 'plaisirs' reminiscent of the plays of the contemporary playwright, Dancourt (1661-1725). His play *Les Trois Cousines* (c. 1696) heavily satirises these pursuits, rather as if Alan Bennett were to write a play about a group of English aristocrats visiting Glyndebourne.

Watteau's art enjoyed a revival of interest in the mid-nineteenth century; Hugo, Banville, Gautier and especially Baudelaire responded to it. The revival was doubtless one element of the more general reaction against an age of materialism, of bourgeois mediocrity, the impulse towards the lowest common denominator of imaginative understanding. It was after all the age which could prosecute *Les Fleurs du mal* and *Madame Bovary*. Poems on the *fête galante* theme were also written by Banville, Gautier and Baudelaire. It is well documented that Verlaine enjoyed Watteau's painting and, especially, responded to the Goncourt brothers' studies of eighteenth-century art. The aristocratic figures have become *commedia* characters:

> Tout un cortège de dames changées en bergères, Colombine, Camargo, ou Pulcinella, de marquis et chevaliers en Arlequin, Pierrot, Scapin et Scaramouche; des abbés un peu 'noirs', un docteur lunaire, un pirate espagnol; leurs négrillons, perruches, singes et animaux familiers; des musiciens aussi, tambourin, luth, guitare. Tout le grand et petit monde, faux et vrai à souhait. (*30*, p. 658)

This is to some point, for an underlying assumption of *Fêtes galantes* is the notion of the mask which conceals the feeling person, 'Jouant du luth et dansant et quasi / Tristes sous leurs déguisements fantasques' ('Clair de lune', 3-4). Above all the onlooking Pierrot of Watteau's painting encapsulates Verlaine's own distancing of himself from the world of emotions which is the substance of *Fêtes galantes* (see *36*). Indeed a number of critics have traced the probable pictorial originals of some of Verlaine's *fête galante* poems (*11, passim, 13,* pp. 209, 220). What matters of course is what Verlaine made of these and doubtless other related inspirations. Clearly he responded to the Watteau who used the artifice of the *fête galante* to explore essential and natural truths of the human condition. Obviously this 'impersonality' would appeal to a young poet still closely identified with the Parnassian movement. Watteau's figures appear to seek harmonious happiness with the right partners; some succeed, some fail. The couples, partners in dance and song, symbolise the psychological truths of harmony and fulfilment; the distant, isolated figures, the absence of this fulfilment. The apparently lighthearted *fête galante* mode explores with complete seriousness the life of the emotions. The paradox does not stop here. This life itself brings with it numerous ambiguities. The very artificiality which has revealed these essential human truths and aspirations also asks the spectator such questions as 'can these scenes of harmony be trusted; is such harmony possible, and if so, how long does it last?' The apparent *légèreté* of the paintings, an aspect too readily seized upon and used to dismiss Watteau, *is* only apparent. We have only to consider the central female figure in *L'Embarquement pour Cythère* moving away from the island, her head turned wistfully towards the paradise she is leaving, to understand this.

Verlaine responded, then, to Watteau's use of the impersonal stylised mode as a means of seriously exploring the intensely personal world of love and its disappointments. Watteau achieves an impersonal, some would say objective, means of studying that which is most personal. He gave Verlaine an example of how he might usefully distance himself from the emotions he knows most intimately; usefully because in *Fêtes galantes* the emotional confusion is located in the conflict between active and passive modes of loving. Hugo's poem, 'La Fête chez Thérèse', probably less influential, evokes an aristocratic country gathering of lovers in the course of which a play is acted by characters of the *commedia dell'arte.* The harmonious atmosphere, when nature and the entire spectacle blend, 'Si bien qu'à ce concert gracieux et classique, / La nature mêlait un peu de sa musique' (57-58), and this at the close of day when the characters' emotions fuse with nature, all this is highly characteristic of Verlaine's *fête galante* mode and is clearly present in the opening poem 'Clair de lune'.

I suggest that *Fêtes galantes* can be considered as a coherent collection of poems with a definite structure, that of an emotional life, much as we find in Hugo's *Les Contemplations* or Baudelaire's *Les Fleurs du mal.* The first and last poems of *Fêtes galantes* ('Clair de lune' and 'Colloque sentimental') function as a kind of framework to the ever-changing picture of emotional life on the canvas of the remaining twenty poems. These two poems operate to achieve a 'distance' comparable to that of Watteau's paintings. This is in no way a verbal transcription of Watteau's mode of painting. 'Clair de lune' is, literally, a scene setter. All the main elements of the collection are present in this poem and indeed the first line 'Votre âme est un paysage choisi', is the key to the collection. Firstly, the landscape is identified with the soul, the poet's and, quite possibly, our own. The scenes depicted in the remaining poems will ultimately be statements about the poet's and our own emotional landscape. Secondly, it is a 'paysage *choisi*'; it has a particularity, a uniqueness, a stylisation; in short, an artificiality which will permit an exploration of the natural life of the emotions. These emotions are embodied, symbolised, in the figures (2-8). The use of the word 'masques' suggests the ambiguity of truth and half-truth which is developed in lines 3-4, 'et quasi / Tristes sous leurs déguisements fantasques'. The brilliant costumes belie the more sombre emotional reality. This is borne out as the poem progresses, 'Ils n'ont pas l'air

de croire à leur bonheur' (7). It is uncertain whether happiness exists, or, if it does, whether it lasts. It is a world of song
and dance (3), the image of harmony, of quintessential experience. However the song, in the 'mode mineur' (5), suggests
sadness and doubt. In verse 3 the scene is transformed by
moonlight into another world. Verlaine has possibly borrowed
this transfiguration by moonlight from Hugo's 'La Fête chez
Thérèse'; certainly he has developed it further, and particularly in the area of sensations. The sounds and movement of
the dancing, singing figures have been transformed into those
of the birds and the fountains. The figures (embodiments of
emotions) have been replaced by elements of nature (symbols
of desire, fulfilment, possible failure). Imagery and symbolism have superseded word painting. So transfiguration operates equally on the poetic art. The emotional landscape has
been explored on a deep, essential level, and doubt has
become pleasure and pain in the cadence strongly suggestive
of simultaneous fulfilment ('extase') and sterility 'marbres':
'Et sangloter d'extase les jets d'eau, / Les grands jets d'eau
sveltes parmi les marbres' (11-12). This 'embodiment' of
sensuous and certainly sensual experience constitutes a major
example of Verlaine's art of symbolist impressionism. Thus,
in 'Clair de lune' a stylised world is established, one which is
then further transformed (verse 3). This is the artificial,
transfigured, self-enclosed *fête galante* world of which the
remaining poems are a part. Never again are we reminded
that this world is the poet's/our own soul. We are invited
once and for all to enter fully into this world.

'Colloque sentimental' repeats the ambiguity of the opening poem. One of the characters in the dialogue appears to
doubt that any part of the couple's experience of 'bonheur'
ever happened. At the very least s/he does not remember.
There is additional uncertainty: the characters seem like
ghosts (6); and by whom are they overheard (16)? It is not
altogether certain they *were* heard. All might equally have
been imagined by the poet/reader. In this sense, then, the
poem casts a further ambiguity, this time retrospective, over
the entire collection. The suggestive power of the emotions is
all the stronger for this uncertainty. In a sense the very

quality of our existence is put in doubt. So equally there may be a move back on the part of the disbelieving character from the enclosed *fête galante* world to a familiar reality. We seek refuge from uncertainty in the certain reality of disbelief. An emotional shift such as this is entirely appropriate to what is ultimately a thematic ambiguity.

In 'L'Art poétique' one of the illustrations which Verlaine gives of his ideal art, 'la chanson grise / Où l'Indécis au Précis se joint' (7-8), is 'des beaux yeux derrière des voiles' (9). It seems to me that the *fête galante* mode is the 'voiles'. That which is half-concealed ('yeux') is the emotional world with which the poems are concerned and to which we now turn.

Each of the poems deals with love from a particular angle. In fact the themes, that is, emotional attitudes towards love, cover a very wide range, from lighthearted enjoyment to despairing isolation. Moreover, these related themes are dealt with in groups of poems, so that a number of aspects of the same theme are offered in a kaleidoscopic presentation. 'Pantomime' and 'Sur l'herbe' give a specifically lighthearted picture of the playfulness of relationships, in Watteauesque terms. The *commedia dell'arte* characters engage in the playful stages of 'l'amour naissant'. Colombine, in 'Pantomime', feels love dawning (10-12). The lover in 'Sur l'herbe' indulges in the stock language of adoring the loved one (7-8). This lightheartedness is picked up later in 'En bateau' in the spoken words of the aristocratic figure who articulates the theme of risk-taking in love:

> C'est l'instant, Messieurs, ou jamais,
> D'être audacieux, et je mets
> Mes deux mains partout désormais!   (4-6)

The landscape and the characters, let us recall, represent the poet's/reader's soul. The risk-taking is that of a person, not merely of a character in a brief narrative poem.

In 'L'Allée', 'A la promenade', 'Dans la grotte', 'Cortège' and 'Les Coquillages', Verlaine intensifies this idealised love game into a stylised sensual idealism which includes the erotic. 'L'Allée' offers a detailed portrait of a woman loosely based on the *blason* device, used in the sixteenth century and dating back, via the poets of the Middle Ages, to Antiquity. It is a device whereby a woman's beauty is detailed from head to toe. In this instance, the woman's appearance is presented firstly from a distance:

> Fardée et peinte comme au temps des bergeries,
> Frêle parmi les nœuds énormes de rubans,
> Elle passe, sous les ramures assombries,　　(1-3)

and then from close up:

> ... Le nez mignon avec la bouche
> Incarnadine, grasse et divine d'orgeuil
> Inconscient.　　(11-13)

In 'A la promenade', the poem following 'L'Allée', the same scene is entered more intimately, for it is presented from the point of view of one of the lovers; the man is reprimanded for his audacity:

> Immensément excessive et farouche,
> On est puni par un regard très sec,
> Lequel contraste, au demeurant, avec
> La moue assez clémente de la bouche.　　(17-20)

'Dans la grotte' employs consciously archaic eighteenth-century poetic diction to express the lover's complete submission to the pain of love in this idealised love world, 'Là! Je me tue à vos genoux! / Car ma détresse est infinie' (1-2). The poem closes with a Petrarchan conceit; the lover asks if he needs a sword with which to kill himself given that his heart has already been pierced with love's arrows from his mistress's eyes. 'Cortège' and 'Les Coquillages' present essentially the same stylised loving in even more elaborate terms. 'Cortège', clearly inspired by Watteau's painting of the same name, nonetheless captures the quintessential artificiality of the scene in such a way that the pet monkey gazing at the woman's *décolletage* and the negro attendant peeping at his mistress's ankles function like sixteenth-century emblems to symbolise repressed desire strong enough to be lust. Such feelings are spoken in the first person in the erotic poem 'Les Coquillages', clearly modelled on eighteenth-century erotic poetry, such as 'Le Sein' from *Tableaux* by Parny. Each shell, we are told, 'A sa particularité' (3). There follows a systematic progression through a set of shell-lover equivalences, beginning with the emotional state of the lovers, 'L'un a la pourpre de nos âmes' (4) and ending thus, 'Mais un, entre autres, me troubla' (13). This refusal to give a physical equivalence coupled with the positioning of this, the closing line, in isolation from the rest of the poem, open up the poem, albeit in a fairly obvious manner, to the erotic of the unspoken, the hinted. As with most erotic art, more than enough clues have already been given.

Matters taken a stage further are presented in the theme of emotional and sensual surrender in 'Les Ingénus', 'Mandoline' and 'En sourdine'. In 'Les Ingénus' Verlaine depicts the emotional surrender in the early stages of a relationship:

Les belles, se pendant rêveuses à nos bras,
Dirent alors des mots si spécieux, tout bas,
Que notre âme, depuis ce temps, tremble et s'étonne. (10-12)

'Mandoline' captures the precise moment when the lovers, their exquisite clothes, their style ('Leur élégance', 11), their happiness, their shadows, all blend perfectly with the moonlight, the music, the quivering breezes. This precise moment of total harmony of sensations, emotions, physicality, is encapsulated in intense movement, 'Tourbillonnent dans l'extase / D'une lune rose et grise' (13-14). As with the 'grands jets d'eau sveltes' ('Clair de lune', 12), this kind of movement appears both momentary and eternal, mobile and static. It is worth noting that in both poems Verlaine uses the word 'extase' to denote emotional and sensual ecstasy. 'En sourdine' treats this ecstasy on a more intimate level. The lover addresses his mistress with commands to surrender the thinking and then the feeling self. The process is easily traced in the verbal imperatives, '*Fondons* nos âmes, nos cœurs / Et nos sens extasiés' (5-6), '*Croise* tes bras sur ton sein' (10), 'Et de ton cœur endormi / *Chasse* à jamais tout dessein' (11-12) and '*Laissons-nous persuader*' (13). It is a systematic process.

With the poem 'Cythère' the ideal world of total surrender is achieved. Cythera, the island of Aphrodite's temple, has long been a favoured subject of painters and poets, Watteau and Baudelaire among them.[2] Verlaine is writing very much within this tradition. The poem's theme is ideal love, a world of passivity, of complete sensual gratification:

> L'odeur des roses, faible, grâce
> Au vent léger d'été qui passe,
> Se mêle aux parfums qu'elle a mis;   (4-6)

There is too the promise of pleasure to come, 'sa lèvre / Communique une exquise fièvre' (8-9). The witty tone of the final verse is a trifle disconcerting in its practicality. Love conquers all, we are told, except hunger. On this island there is also food, albeit of a rather insubstantial nature, which 'Nous préservent des courbatures' (12). This somewhat self-deprecatory wit is, in a sense, a negation or at least a qualification of the idealism, much as Watteau's *Le Pèlerinage à l'isle de Cythère* has been subjected to discussion as to whether the figures are going to or leaving the island (*39*, pp. 399-400). At the very least, the idealism is cynical and recalls that of Baudelaire in 'Un Voyage à Cythère'. Furthermore, this qualification, admittedly mild, prefigures that, more marked, in 'En sourdine', when, at the moment of surrender, the lovers' despair is heard in the nightingale's song (19-20).

The theme of love has so far been presented as a mainly positive and pleasurable experience. Nonetheless, love's less attractive aspects are at least hinted at in some of these poems, 'Cythère' for example. Other poems deal more directly with these issues. For instance the idealised love scene in

---

[2] See for instance Watteau's *L'Embarquement pour Cythère* and, an ironical and bitter treatment, Baudelaire's 'Un Voyage à Cythère' in *Les Fleurs du mal* (*10*), pp. 117-19.

'Pantomime' opens with the picture of Pierrot very pragmatically having a good meal. We are *told* he is practical, 'Et, pratique, entame un pâté' (3). The Interpreting from the archetypal *commedia* scenario, Pierrot has either been rejected by Colombine in favour of Arlequin, or he has realised he would not even be able to compete successfully with Arlequin. Pierrot's practicality, then, suggests a hardening of the heart in order to cope with the situation, and so a degree of isolation and non-communication.[3] It is in contrast with Colombine's soft feelings of love. Indeed the entire situation is mimed, as the title suggests. Nowhere in the poem does verbal communication take place. Nor does it in 'Lettre' where the lover / poet uses the eighteenth-century epistolary poetic form to address his mistress. The letter form alone suggests isolation and possibly an attendant despair, as does the use of the Petrarchan conceit of death in life in 'Dans la grotte' (11-12), which gives the poem an alternative, grimmer meaning.

Moreover, love does not last. The longest poem, 'En patinant', uses the familiar device of the passing seasons to depict the passing of love. In this poem there is a further dimension, the idea of manipulation. The poem opens with the assertion: 'Nous fûmes dupes, vous et moi, / Des manigances mutuelles' (1-2). While this is redeemed by the more lighthearted closing lines, the lovers will win through and 'nos / Parieurs tremblent pour leur bourse' (57-58); at the very least a note of despair sounds through the poem, which could make the closing lines seem factitious.

Failure, despair, and fear are dealt with more directly in 'Le Faune', 'L'amour par terre' and 'Colloque sentimental'. Like its more positive counterpart, 'Mandoline', 'Le Faune' fixes the precise moment when the lover realises that love

---

[3] J. Starobinski (*Portrait de l'artiste en saltimbanque,* Geneva, Skira, 1970) notes that nineteenth-century painters and writers used Pierrot, the earthbound, obtuse clown to symbolise man's despair at woman's triumph over him. From this developed the more familiar figure of the tragic clown who is aware of his failures, ironies and the ephemerality of the human condition, and which the Pierrot figure gazing out of Watteau's *Les Plaisirs du bal* seems to prefigure.

will not last. The 'instants sereins' (4) have been followed by
'cette heure dont la fuite / Tournoie au son des tambourins'
(7-8). The word 'Tournoie' is related to the word used in
'Mandoline', 'Tourbillonnent' (13). These words closely associated with musical instruments, respectively, 'tambourins'
and 'mandoline' suggest strongly the harsher and softer
aspects of love, and particularly the exact moment of deep
awareness. As with 'jets d'eau' in 'Clair de lune', the movement is again both momentary and eternal, mobile and
apparently static. 'L'Amour par terre' is more or less an
allegory. The statue of love has been dashed from its pedestal
overnight by strong winds. The poet reflects on this scene,
'Oh! c'est triste de voir debout le piédestal / Tout seul!'
(9-10). While, thankfully, the poet does not dwell on the
obvious sexual symbolism, he does express his 'pensers mé-
lancoliques' (10). They concern 'un avenir solitaire et fatal'
(12). The word 'fatal' introduces the idea of destiny, the
certainty of passing love, and so, of loneliness. The fear
expressed in 'Le Faune' apparently has some justification.
The extreme doubt and negativity of 'Colloque sentimental' has been discussed. With its suggestion of the apparent
indifference of the woman and its consistent use of deliberate
archaisms of vocabulary and syntax ('hormis', 'astre', 'est-ce
pas') redolent of the eighteenth century, the poem distances
the *entire* experience expressed in the collection, and puts it
into doubt. As such it is perhaps the most despairing poem
of all.

Despair of love lasting is polarised into the themes of
innocence and corruption in 'Fantoches' and 'Colombine'. In
'Fantoches' the evil *commedia* characters Scaramouche and
Polichinelle seemingly plot in the moonlight while Colombine steals away to her handsome lover. Love asserts itself
over evil and, it is hoped, will assuage the lovers' distress. In
'Colombine', on the other hand, Colombine is presented as
an evil manipulator of her innocent lovers:

Oh! dis-moi vers quels
Mornes ou cruels
Désastres

> L'implacable enfant ...

>> Conduit son troupeau
>> De dupes?   (28-31; 35-36)

The idea of destiny too is introduced in the word 'fatidique':

>> –Eux ils vont toujours!
>> Fatidique cours
>>> Des astres   (25-27)

The rhyming of 'Des astres' with its homonym and etymological offspring 'Désastres' (30) underlines the point.

Across the collection, the distinctive theme of love is developed in an equally distinctive way. There is a deepening emotional richness. In general the poems up to 'En patinant' are fairly straightforward depictions of a happy, lighthearted love. 'En patinant' marks a turning point; with the theme of manipulation, the darker side of love is introduced. From this point on, the poems are more complex with the additional dimension of the more negative aspects of love discussed above (see pp. 34-36). This interplay of positive and negative aspects of love, I suggest, is the source of the richness of the later poems as of the essential thematic progression.

If we take together the three *commedia*/Watteauesque poems, 'Pantomime', 'Fantoches' and 'Colombine', it is possible to see this symbolised in the way the character of Colombine is developed. In 'Pantomime', Colombine is surprised by love; she is tender and gentle. In 'Fantoches' she actively seeks her lover, whilst in 'Colombine' she has become a cruel manipulator, she is active rather than passive, and this activity is perceived as malign. As a *commedia* character, she symbolises, from a safe distance, somewhat in the manner of Watteau's artificiality, the range of emotions associated with love and which *Fêtes galantes* explores. As a character associated with love, the Colombine figure may be considered to represent the increasingly complex treatment of love across the collection.

'A la promenade', 'A Clymène' and 'Les Indolents' suggest
a *modus vivendi* in the face of this despair, this 'fate'. As the
title suggests, 'Les Indolents' puts the proposed solution at its
starkest:

> −Bah! malgré les destins jaloux,
> Mourons ensemble, voulez-vous?
> −La proposition est rare.
>
> −Le rare est le bon. Donc mourons.   (1-4)

The stance adopted with its logic, 'Le rare est le bon. Donc
mourons' is specifically amoral with its implied (conventional) equation of death with sex. The tone of the poem is
no less so:

> −Hi! hi! hi! quel amant bizarre!
>
> −Bizarre, je ne sais. Amant
> Irréprochable, assurément.   (6-8)

'A la promenade' and 'A Clymène' approach the theme of
amorality from a different angle. In 'A la promenade' we are
told quite simply that the lovers are 'Cœurs tendres, mais
affranchis du serment' (10). As in Watteau's paintings, they
are absolved of all responsibilities and are free to pursue their
pleasures, their search for the right partner in defiance of fate.
The lived reality of such a world is the theme of the beautiful
poem, 'A Clymène'. As in 'En sourdine' the poem traces the
process of invoking passivity, of relaxing control. This time
the power of the loved one is specifically in the domain of
sensations. Here too Verlaine self-consciously uses Baudelairian *correspondances* (18). (Baudelaire's sonnet 'Correspondances' (*10,* vol. I, p. 11) explores the symbolic connections
of perfume, sound and colour.) In 'A Clymène' the effect on
the poet's senses, backed up by the 'authority' of another
poet's experience, is offered as a *justification* of the poet's
surrender. The repeated construction 'Puisque' leading to the
final 'Ainsi soit-il!' (20) which, translated, means 'Amen',
has, as in 'Les Indolents', a semblance of logic. In addition
the strikingly liturgical quality of the verse seems to offer

further justification. Amorality, then, a refusal of responsibility, some would say decadence, a seizing of the moment, is both an aspect of love and may well be a way of dealing with love's transience. The 'Ainsi soit-il' which closes 'A Clymène' is more than the quasi-religious acquiescent welcoming of love that it may first appear to be. As I have suggested above, the syntax of 'Puisque ... Ainsi soit-il' offers a justification, a legitimisation of amorality. The world of 'Les Indolents' operates on just such a legitimised assumption. Interestingly a comparable 'logic' is used, 'Le rare est le bon. Donc mourons / Comme dans les Décamérons' (4-5). The reference to Boccaccio's *Decameron,* courtly tales of love and intrigue, seemingly legitimises this attitude further. For all its apparently sophisticated lightheartedness, the poem touches on the extremes of love and death which have little connection with the love and death of the Petrarchan conceit in 'Dans la grotte'. In 'Les Indolents' the game is deadly serious.

A critic has referred to this amorality as 'libertinage sophistiqué'.[4] This seems to me accurate, but I believe the amorality to be a great deal more than this. As such it is the principle connection with Verlaine's vision of love in *Romances sans paroles.* In 'Les Ingénus' the amoral is specifically a freedom from commitment, 'affranchis du serment' ('A la promenade', 10). It may equally be viewed as a special world where such commitments are irrelevant, if not rejected. Certainly this last attitude would constitute the darker side of freedom. Another way of considering the matter would be to suggest that it is a world of irresponsibility, attempted, if not chosen. The amoral, then, may usefully be seen as the irresponsible. Verlaine's investigation of the nature of love has led him to the verge of taking responsibility, a point beyond which he has chosen not to go. The amoral *fête galante* world strongly and permanently hints at a world of irresponsibility as a way of life.

It is in this context that I want to suggest that beneath the overt theme of love there lies a theme less directly expressed;

---

[4] M. Barlow, *Poésies, Verlaine,* Profil d'une œuvre, 79 (Paris, Hatier, 1982), p. 26.

it is the theme of passivity. Each poem can be seen as an evocation of a state of passivity. In a fundamental sense this is the key to Verlaine's poetic vision and art. This theme is *suggested* throughout the collection and is the mood through which the dominant theme of love is filtered. In Verlaine's case the evocation of states of passivity may usefully be viewed as the aesthetic counterpart of his own lived refusal to take responsibility for himself, his actions, his moods, his decisions. It is an astounding and, in some ways, a horrendous transmutation of lived experience into art. The impossible lands of *Fêtes galantes,* as indeed of *Romances sans paroles,* have their genesis in that which is only too possible.

As with the theme of love, the states of passivity cover a wide range. 'Les Coquillages', 'Dans la grotte' and 'A Clymène' evoke the pleasure of letting go, of achieving the perfect passivity of physical pleasure. As suggested, the theme of 'En sourdine' is the process of bringing about a state of passivity, here a form of receptivity to nature, in such a way that the individual and nature become one on some plane of exquisite pleasure, which is detailed further in 'A Clymène'. J.-P. Richard refers to this process as the removal of 'le moi conscient' (*32,* pp. 165-85 *passim*), of the thinking self, to allow the world of sensations alone to come into being. Passivity too can be discerned in the theme of manipulation; the victims are passive in 'En patinant'. Passivity is equally the inability or refusal to do anything about this manipulation and the resultant isolation ('Fantoches'). It is vulnerability in 'En bateau', fear and loss of control over one's destiny ('Le Faune'). Above all, in 'A la promenade', 'A Clymène' and 'Les Indolents', passivity is manifested in amorality which is legitimised into a way of life in the *fête galante* world; refusal of commitment is proposed as an ethos. It is a serious proposition and one which Verlaine explores much further in *Romances sans paroles.*

This layering of themes, one overt, one suggested, is, of course, appropriate to the presentation of mainly non-intellectual themes. I want to go further and suggest that the *way* the themes are presented also emerges as a theme in its own right. These structures are the nearest the poems get to being 'intellectual'. After all, the world of emotions has to be set down. For the sake of clarity, four distinctive modes of presenting the emotions can be discerned.

Firstly, in 'Pantomime' and 'A la promenade', for instance, Verlaine uses the device of contrast. Pierrot's practical activity of eating is contrasted with Colombine's passive reception of love to underline the theme of isolation, and the contrast between callousness and feeling, corruption and innocence, conventional masculine and feminine principles. The word 'contraste' is actually used in 'A la promenade' to emphasise the enigmatically playful quality of idealised love scene. The woman's cold gaze is contrasted with her generous smile:

> On est puni par un regard très sec,
> Lequel contraste, au demeurant, avec
> La moue assez clémente de la bouche.   (18-20)

This contrast between appearance and reality is tightened into a paradox in a number of poems, notably 'L'Allée' and 'Dans la grotte'. Paradox, the second mode, is obviously of the essence of the *fête galante* world, dealing as it does with artificial appearance and emotional truth. 'L'Allée', which precedes 'A la promenade', is a purely external portrait of the lovers of the latter poem. The woman is virtually masked, 'Fardée et peinte comme au temps des bergeries' (1). It is seemingly impossible to know her as a person. In this sense the poem is a fruitless attempt to discover her, to resolve the paradox of appearance and truth. One *truth* is understood, 'la bouche / Incarnadine, grasse et divine d'orgueil / Inconscient' (11-13). It is of course a further paradox. The woman's arrogance is unconscious and this gives her mouth simultaneously a goddess-like and sensual quality. Arrogance, and unconscious arrogance at that, is one of the most difficult emotions to penetrate. The *rejet* of 'Incarnadine', echoed by that of 'Inconscient', stresses the physical and emotional qualities in such a way as to suggest an equivalent and, I would say, a symbol. However, the red mouth is not a straightforward symbol of unconscious arrogance, an interesting manifestation of amorality. It could equally symbolise its

opposite, a direct sensuality not admitted to. This paradox-
ical symbolic import of the physical and emotional, the
uncertainty as to which symbolises which, echoes that of
'grasse et divine d'orgueil' in an effect like a hall of mirrors.
Is pride sensuality or something divine? What exactly are the
relations between the polarities 'grasse' and 'divine' and *their*
relationship to 'orgueil'? There is no one clear answer. This
itself is a quality of the woman's personality which can never
be known. As suggested above 'Dans la grotte' employs the
Petrarchan paradox of death by love, and so life in death and
death in life. It is a familiar poetic device setting up a 'hall of
mirrors' of endless paradoxes which captures the insolubility
of enslavement by love, and which is further enriched by
Verlaine's playing on the tradition of courtly love whereby
'to die', in a love poem in particular, meant 'to have sex'.

'A Cythère', 'Mandoline' and 'En sourdine' present a
world within the world of *Fêtes galantes,* the third mode. 'A
Cythère' is the pure, perfect world of sensations. This plane
of rarefied existence is doubtless the world experienced, in
movement, by the characters in 'Mandoline' as they 'Tourbillonnent dans l'extase' (13). In its more relaxed form this
world is that to which the lovers aspire in 'En sourdine'. The
title, signifying a muted instrument (metaphorically it can
mean 'secretly', which would not be inappropriate here),
gives some idea of the quality of this other plane of existence.

It is, however, an impossible land. Verlaine does not
become aware of this, it seems, until 'En sourdine'. As the
lovers approach total passivity, relaxation, and, we are told,
'Voix de notre désespoir, / Le rossignol chantera' (19-20), an
opposite emotion emerges. This, the fourth mode, I term a
dialectic. In the abstract, dialectic may be defined as follows:
one emotional state is taken to the extreme point where it
brings into being its opposite emotion. This is comparable to
the essence of Mallarmé's Symbolist undertaking, 'après avoir
trouvé le Néant, j'ai trouvé le Beau';[5] it is only by encounter-

---

[5] Letter to Henri Cazalis, S. Mallarmé, *Correspondance 1862-71* (Paris,
Gallimard, 1959), p. 220.

ing total negation that the poet can imagine its opposite, 'l'Idéal'. Verlaine's dialectic, of course, operates on an emotional level. The happiness in 'En sourdine' cannot last. In addition, the letting go of the thinking self runs so close to self-annihilation that the conscious self reasserts itself. And this takes the form of despair in 'En sourdine', despair at the loss of the conscious self, or equally at not being able to escape its control, at not being able to achieve the emotional ideal of total passivity. Certainly there is too the despair of the deeper parts of the emotional self which are usually suppressed.

A comparison with Baudelaire's 'Parfum exotique' will perhaps clarify Verlaine's use of a dialectic mode to present emotional states. Both 'En sourdine' and 'Parfum exotique' convey the experience of relaxing and opening up the world of the senses. Both poems use the device of synaesthesia, whereby one sense impression conjures up further sense impressions in an endless chain reaction of sensations, an increasingly complex and self-contained world of associations, another plane of existence, in fact. 'Parfum exotique' reaches a goal, conveyed in the intricate mingling of sensations, 'Pendant que le parfum des verts tamariniers / ... Se mêle dans mon âme au chant des mariniers' (12, 14). Baudelaire's poem is an exercise in the powers of the sensual imagination. His acute awareness of despair is contained in such texts as the 'Spleen' poems in *Les Fleurs du mal.* Baudelaire polarises his awareness of the inherent impossibility of creating a superior world into separate kinds of poem, poems of despair ('Spleen' poems) and poems of elation (for instance 'Parfum exotique'), each exploring a network of sense impressions, linked with one another, and symbolising a particular state of mind. Verlaine, on the other hand, explores within the same poem these contradictions. 'En sourdine' does not achieve a goal. Instead it demonstrates the limits to which that particular emotional state can be pushed. The risks Verlaine takes are no less courageous than Baudelaire's for being different.

On a more mundane level, a mode of presentation such as this conveys the understandable fear that happiness will not last. 'Le Faune' demonstrates this very clearly. There is too, something here of the dynamic of the self-fulfilling prophecy. Each of these suggested approaches has its truth. Not surprisingly, there is overall a greater incidence of this dialectical presentation of the theme in the second half of the collection ('Mandoline', 'A Clymène', 'Les Indolents', 'Colombine', 'En sourdine'), which is obviously a factor in the greater complexity noted in the thematic development of the collection.

I suggested earlier that the way the theme is presented constitutes a theme in its own right. The three 'layers' of themes in *Fêtes galantes,* love, passivity and the mode of presentation, blend in 'En sourdine'. Here the willed gradual surrender and resultant despair, which is nothing other than vulnerability, is a dialectical process. Emotions work like this. The world of 'En sourdine' is more recognisable than that of 'Cythère' for instance. In 'En sourdine' we are invited to participate in the gradual process of passivity, in 'Cythère' to witness an idealised world. This art of merging layers in 'En sourdine' marks an important link with the poetic art of *Romances sans paroles.*

The significant connections between *Fêtes galantes* and *Romances sans paroles* are the themes of love and passivity, their links with the positing of an amoral world where responsibility is refused, and the expression of this in a form of pure poetry. As such *Fêtes galantes* contains elements of this, Verlaine's art of symbolist impressionism. By using the *fête galante* mode, Verlaine has explored these issues in a safe, detached way. He distances himself from the highly personal and confused emotions to clarify the conflict between active and passive modes of loving. In *Romances sans paroles* the same issues are examined in a more personal way, and so, more deeply. In so far as 'En sourdine' expresses the experience of willed passivity more intimately than the other poems in the collection, it is the key connecting poem between the two collections. In *Fêtes galantes,* Verlaine is an onlooker, gazing at the Watteauesque painterly poems which he creates. He is a spectator. In *Romances sans paroles,* the more specifically musical poems, Verlaine is more profoundly engaged. 'En sourdine', with its stated musicality, points the way.

2
Themes in
Romances sans paroles

As with *Fêtes galantes,* the themes of *Romances sans paroles* are predominantly emotional states. To the familiar themes of love and passivity is added that of freedom. In this chapter I shall consider three ways in which *Romances sans paroles* develops from *Fêtes galantes*; firstly, the use of the *Romances sans paroles* mode with its subdivisions, secondly the resultant double perspective of external reality and inner emotional reality which permeates the collection, and finally how the presentation of the themes focuses the conflict noted in *Fêtes galantes* between active and passive ways of loving into the issue of responsibility versus irresponsibility, the issue which, I believe, accounts for the uneven quality of the poetry in this collection. There is, quite simply, a marked contrast between a 'poésie pure' of delicious passivity, free from moral values, a poetry of presentation (as distinct from representation), and a poetry of unsubtly expressed emotions, clearly autobiographical in nature. *Fêtes galantes* presents a wholly imagined inner world where ethos and emotional state are unified in the specifically pure, amoral world of 'A la promenade', 'A Clymène' and 'Les Indolents'. In *Romances sans paroles* this is not the case. *Romances sans paroles* explores further the *fête galante* world and, as it were, tests out these imaginary lands. As we shall discover, the lands are visited and yet it is impossible to remain there. Emotions and ethos are ultimately found to be in conflict. This is because Verlaine is forever torn between the pull of freedom and the temptation of security, and refuses to *choose* one or the other. I consider that this unresolved gap between the delicious emotional state, its pain as well as its pleasure, and the ethical basis on which it is founded, generates the best and worst of Verlaine's poetic art and is the hallmark of *Romances sans paroles*. In view of this it seems to me crucial to adopt two approaches to the collection: firstly that of 'poésie pure', poetry in its own right, and secondly a biographical approach in the case of a number of poems, specifically the fourth and sixth 'Ariettes oubliées', 'Birds in the night', 'Child wife', 'A Poor Young Shepherd' and 'Beams'. Apart from the 'Ariettes oubliées', these poems contain little that I consider to be of purely aesthetic merit. They are largely versified self-pity and/or anger directed towards Mathilde.

In *Fêtes galantes* Verlaine dealt with the themes of love, passivity and amorality in a detached way, through the *fête galante* world. *Romances sans paroles* is distinctly less detached in its treatment of these themes. In the place of the *fête galante* framework there is the mode of the *Romances sans paroles,* wordless songs, which are subdivided into 'Ariettes oubliées', 'Paysages belges', 'Simples fresques' and 'Aquarelles', that is, musical as well as pictorial modes, linked by the notion of the significance of the unexpressed. While *Romances sans paroles* clearly refers to Mendelssohn's 'Songs without words', the 'Romance' is also a sung elegy, emotional in substance and without complicated dramatic presentation. The genre itself conveys the idea of musicality, of experiences that transcend the limitations of words, a questioning of the power of words, as Chaussivert suggests, a 'remise en question de la parole' (*17*, p. 60). There is too the idea that there is no name for the experience which *Romances sans paroles* collectively portrays. This is less to do with morality, or its absence, than to suggest the uniqueness of a love affair, of which homosexuality is but one element. In short, another plane of existence is involved, as in *Fêtes galantes*. In *Fêtes galantes* this world of delicious passivity was lived vicariously through the *commedia* characters, with the notable exception of 'En sourdine' where the experience is considerably less limited by the specific figures. In *Fêtes galantes* there is an outer reality, that of the *fête galante* world, and an inner reality, the truth of human emotions. With *Romances sans paroles* the outer reality is the fact and circumstances of the relationship with Rimbaud, and Mathilde; the inner reality, the intimate experience of this relationship, what it felt like. The experience is neither vicarious nor transposed beyond recognition. Both realities are the poet's. There is, then, no one clear mode to give specificity to the experience. On the contrary, like music, it is evoked in the very process of its unfolding. 'En sourdine' came nearest to this kind of poetry in *Fêtes galantes*. The mode of the *Romances sans paroles* is entirely appropriate to this art of symbolist impressionism which presents, not represents.

Within this overall genre it seems to me worth considering the titles of the separate sections. 'Ariettes oubliées', the first section, contains the quintessentially Verlainian poetry. The 'Ariette' certainly refers to the musical comedy, *Ninette à la cour,* by the eighteenth-century dramatist, Favart, from which the opening epigram is taken. Rimbaud discovered these plays in the library at Charleville. As the name implies, an 'Ariette' is a small aria. Its distinctive quality is an unaccompanied melody. The melody is the theme, that is, the ephemeral quality of the emotions, possibly a reason for the use of the diminutive. The melody's accompaniment derives from the words' rich suggestiveness, connotative, phonological and metrical. Given the fact that Verlaine named this particular section later (they were originally to have been called *Romances sans paroles*), there is, as Bornecque suggests (*12,* pp. 97-113, *passim*), a retrospective view; the experience of the relationship, of its emotional essence, has been *forgotten* by Rimbaud.

'Paysages belges' obviously recalls the setting of *Fêtes galantes,* 'Votre âme est un paysage choisi' ('Clair de lune'). The equivalence between landscape and emotions now applies in reverse; the Belgian landscape is that of the poet's soul, it is seen through the poet's emotional being. This section is a continuation of the emotional world of 'Ariettes oubliées' and is more outward looking. The subdivision, 'Simples fresques' (fresco art implies painting directly on to wet plaster), suggests the seizing of the bare essential elements of the experience, in the form of sparse landscape details. It is the art of the precise nuance and of the rapid gesture. 'Aquarelles' continues the painting mode. The water colours may be considered the visual equivalent of 'Ariettes oubliées'. The pictorial detail of the landscape is fused with the emotional landscape. There is a shift in emphasis from music in the first section, to painting in the final section, which denotes a move away from the completely personal world of emotions and sensations in its complex unfolding process ('C'est l'extase', 'Ariette' I) to a world where details from a 'recognisable' external world depict a particular emotional attitude ('Green').

Some of these attitudes, in 'Aquarelles', are surprisingly dogmatic ('Child wife') and link up with the curious poem 'Birds in the night'. The title, probably taken from a lullaby by Sullivan, recalls Verlaine's use of bird symbolism for distressed states of mind, for example the nightingale in 'En sourdine', 'Voix de notre désespoir, / Le rossignol chantera' (19-20) and the crow in the eighth 'Ariette' (17). The symbolic associations with distress remind us that Verlaine's original title for the collection was *La Mauvaise Chanson* with its emphasis on self-pity, and its obvious contrast with *La Bonne Chanson*. As Verlaine wrote to Hugo, 'C'est moi le quitté' (*8*, vol. III, p. 143). Appearances are irrelevant, Verlaine felt abandoned; Mathilde's separation order hurt, presumably because she took some decisive control of the situation. The genre of the popular song indicated by the title, 'Birds in the night', is appropriate to the poem which stands alone and brash in its directness, in its channelling of strong emotions towards Mathilde. It can belong to no other section in the collection apart from 'Aquarelles' which it prefigures, in particular the poems 'Child wife', 'A Poor Young Shepherd' and 'Beams'. All four poems depict a strong emotion in a forceful way which refuses any subtle nuances.

Each section is linked with a place visited by Verlaine and Rimbaud. 'Paysages belges' obviously recalls Belgium, 'Birds in the night' and 'Aquarelles' are from the London experience, while 'Ariettes oubliées' probably covers the entire experience, certainly the early Paris-based relationship, and that on a far more essential level. It is the 'paysage intérieur' of merging emotions and sensations, Verlaine's own *Cythère,* the journey to and from the island of ideal love. A number of critics assign each section to a particular person in Verlaine's life at this time. The general consensus appears to be thus: 'Ariettes oubliées' – nostalgia for Mathilde; 'Paysages belges' – Rimbaud; and 'Aquarelles' – return to Mathilde. I see an emotional truth and logic in this. After all, Verlaine found it difficult to leave Mathilde and presumably to live, for him, a more adult, homosexual life. On balance, though, I believe the sections signify in a different manner. Each division presents a different location for a particular stage in the relationship with Rimbaud, beginning with the self-enclosed world of emotions ('Ariettes'), the life of adventure in Belgium ('Paysages belges') and then London ('Aquarelles'). Cutting across these sections is the conflict between the reluctance to leave Mathilde and security, and the tempting freedom with Rimbaud. Verlaine's attacks on Mathilde are, after all, externalised fear and cowardice. The straightforward circumstantial adventure is accompanied by a far more complex refusal of this freedom. Even so, each section has its own coherence, recalling the 'blocks' of poems in *Fêtes galantes* (see above, p. 31); for instance 'Ariettes oubliées' presents kaleidoscopic perspectives on the physical, emotional and artistic relationship, ranging from sensual pleasure (I) through the 'morality' of the situation (IV), to regret at the loss of the stable conventional marriage that freedom has demanded (VII).

The collection as a whole has rather less coherence. There is the overall pattern of a decline in emotional intensity and subtlety. The collection begins with the exquisite 'C'est l'extase', the assertion of the reality of the least tangible of experiences, and ends with 'Beams', with its theme of surrender in love. However, in 'Beams' the presentation is utterly conventional and Hugolian in tone. There are two possible explanations for the decline. Firstly, the inevitable diminution of intense experience. Secondly, there may well be some cynical mockery, ever the perspective of Verlaine in exile. Certainly a poem such as 'Beams' bears a strong resemblance to the less impressive poems from *La Bonne Chanson* and later *Sagesse*. Whatever the truth of the matter, the fact remains that the poetry in *Romances sans paroles* ranges from the exquisite to the banal and the ludicrous.

It seems to me too that a double perspective operates. Just as the *fête galante* world, by its very nature, ultimately doubts the existence of the harmony it depicts, so *Romances sans paroles* is pervaded by an atmosphere of retrospective fatalistic melancholy, a strong sense of past, present, and future preconditioned by the past, far more marked than in *Fêtes galantes* (cf. 'Le Faune', 'L'Amour par terre'). Accordingly there is a greater awareness of the gap between ideal and reality than in *Fêtes galantes*. In 'C'est l'extase', for instance, the moment of sublime happiness is immediately questioned 'C'est la nôtre, n'est-ce pas?' (15). Many of the poems are permeated by this fatalistic doubt. Some are entirely composed of it, for instance the eighth 'Ariette', 'Dans l'interminable...' From the beginning in *Romances sans paroles* there is the certainty that harmonious happiness will not last. In the light of this and for the sake of clarity, I shall discuss each section separately with respect to the treatment of the themes of love, passivity and freedom.

In 'Ariettes oubliées' the theme of love is not articulated as such. Instead the poems variously explore finely nuanced facets of the state of being in love. The theme of passivity too pervades this section in the sense that, with the exception of IV, the poems are about a sensual and emotional state in which the poet finds himself. The theme of passivity is united with the theme of freedom, for the poems evoke an attitude of complete surrender, a letting go, including the fearful dimensions of such a situation. Together, then, the nine 'Ariettes' present the essence of the Verlainian emotion of total surrender to love; each poem constitutes an aspect of the entire experience which is thus unfolded in its finely nuanced, ever-changing process. The 'Ariette', 'C'est l'extase' is one of the best examples of this. The exclusively sensual and emotional ecstasy has a life of its own, shown in the use of the impersonal 'C'est' which is coupled with that of the present tense. Moreover, the poem begins *in medias res*; there is no building up to ecstasy as there is, for instance, in Baudelaire's 'Parfum exotique', or indeed Verlaine's 'Cythère' (*Fêtes galantes*). This state of being is explored further in II, which conveys the spiritual dimension of the experience, 'Je devine,

à travers un murmure, / Le contour subtil des voix anciennes'
(1-2). Key words are picked up from I. 'Voix', 'âme', 'antienne' have become 'Le contour subtil des voix anciennes'.
'Voix' denotes an intimacy of communication, 'Anciennes'
echoing 'antienne' in its eternal, pure quality. However, with
the word 'âme' the situation in both poems becomes problem-
atical. In the first 'Ariette' the poet insistently asks for
reassurance, 'Cette âme qui se lamente ... C'est la nôtre, n'est-
ce pas? / La mienne, dis, et la tienne' (13, 15-16). In II, 'âme'
is now specifically distinguished from 'cœur', 'Et mon âme et
mon cœur en délires / Ne sont plus qu'une espèce d'œil
double' (5-6). At the precise moment of discord between soul
and heart, the resultant double perspective is simultaneously
an awareness of love's ephemerality and, ironically ('hélas!'),
a glimpse of perfection:

> ... une espèce d'œil double
> Où tremblote à travers un jour trouble
> L'ariette, hélas! de toutes lyres!   (6-8)

The reference to 'ariette' and 'lyres' posits a link between this
kind of poetry and this type of experience, as if to suggest that
the 'Ariette' were the only way to express the experience.
    Faced with the failure to achieve ideal love, 'Amour pâle,
une aurore future' (4), the poet seeks further passivity, 'O
mourir de cette escarpolette!' (12). It is a very particular kind
of passivity. The swing symbolises the precarious balance
between time past and time to come, youth and age, Rimbaud and Verlaine, of sexual relations, the perfect moment
and the inevitably imperfect existence that ensues. The poet,
then, knowingly wills oblivion in this precarious state of
affairs. More prosaically, he chooses the impossible. There is
no turning back from the torturous situation. In this context,
the opening words 'Je devine' take on the meaning of acute
receptivity. It is the kind of receptivity that leads to a chosen
paralysis of will. The deadly situation is preferable to a dead
life without the relationship. He wants the swing always to
move, an image which recalls that of the 'Jets d'eau' of 'Clair

de lune' in *Fêtes galantes*. The swing is to have the fountains' apparent stasis, the illusion of permanence.

Just as the first poem evoked sensual perfection and doubts, and the second a spiritual ideal and certain doubts, so poem III completes this opening cycle of experience. It is a poem of melancholy. The tragedy is that the poet does not know why he is so desolate:

> C'est bien la pire peine
> De ne savoir pourquoi
> Sans amour et sans haine
> Mon cœur a tant de peine!   (13-16)

This, the essence of despair, has an unresolved quality which focuses and expresses directly that of I, the demand for reassurance, and of II, the certainty of imperfection.

Together, the first three 'Ariettes' convey the entire and extreme range of Verlaine's experience, which is consistently presented as an unfolding process: we are taken through the process with the poet. The remaining 'Ariettes' are rather more varied in that they treat specific aspects of this experience and differ considerably in tone. With the possible exception of VI, poems IV-IX deal with the various forms of pain the relationship inevitably entails. In poem IV the poet demands forgiveness for his way of life, 'Il faut, voyez-vous, nous pardonner les choses' (1). It is a singularly forceful demand for Verlaine and suggests the irresistibility and the difficulty of the life of freedom, understandably perceived as an exile (8). With poems V and VII the pain is specifically that of leaving Mathilde. Following the emotional pattern of I (emotion and questioning), poem V ('Le piano que baise...') beautifully evokes with great subtlety the emotional and physical sensation of hearing, possibly in memory, the sound of a piano in a room filled with a woman's perfume. The second verse queries the source of this sound/memory, 'Qu'as-tu voulu, fin refrain incertain' (10). The past tense suggests that the moment of knowing the answer has already passed, and the poet's inability, or refusal, to find out. Once more the situation is unresolved. Poem VII is far more straightforward, 'O triste, triste était mon âme / A cause, à

cause d'une femme' (1-2). It is straightforward even in its lack
of resolution:

> Mon âme dit à mon cœur: Sais-je
> Moi-même que nous veut ce piège
>
> D'être présents bien qu'exilés,
> Encore que loin en allés?   (13-16)

The split between the soul and heart in poem II at least shows
an understanding of the dilemma of ending a relationship, the
difficulty of being separated and not separate. Here there is
no understanding. Accordingly the 'escarpolette' (II) of exile
is trenchantly summed up in the poet's disbelief, 'Est-il
possible, – le fût-il, – / Ce fier exil, ce triste exil?' (11-12). The
contrast between the present tense ('est-il') and the literary
form of the conditional ('le fût-il'), a kind of partial conjuga-
tion of the verb 'être', simultaneously conveys the poet's
pained incredulity and his attempts to grasp and accept the
loss of his loved one.

'Ariette' VI is of quite a different order. It is Verlaine's
version of Rimbaud's 'Ma Bohème', a half mocking poem of
joyous wandering. Both poets use the same word, 'frou-frou'
(18). As with Rimbaud's poem, Verlaine presents a tenderly
mocking self-portrait. He is a starveling poet out on his great
adventure (25-28). It is a poetic adventure, for he is a 'Petit
poète jamais las / De la rime non attrapée!...' (27-28). He
shows a disconcertingly mature self-awareness, underlined by
the syntactical repetition, '... jamais fatigué / D'être inattentif
et naïf' (30-31).

In poems VIII and IX the pain is presented respectively as
a state of being and in the form of a forceful semi-allegory.
Verlaine's use of personification in VIII:

> Dans l'interminable
> Ennui de la plaine
> La neige incertaine
> Luit comme du sable.   (1-4)

is one of the best examples of Verlaine's art of blending the
emotional and the physical landscape. The depression is total

and the poet's distress is symbolised in the wheezy crow and starving wolves (17-20). Like poem VI, poem IX is more straightforward and has some of the emotional force of poem IV in that it is openly an elaboration on the epigraph from the early seventeenth-century writer Cyrano de Bergerac. A nightingale, seeing its reflection in the river below, is afraid of falling in, although it is safely perched in a tree. Verlaine makes symbolic elaborations on this scene, for example, the reflections of turtle doves in the branches are 'Tes espérances noyées!' (8). The poem is forceful too in its use of Baudelairian semi-allegory, 'Combien, ô voyageur, ce paysage blême / Te mira blême toi-même' (5-6). This poem is the 'Colloque sentimental' of the first section with its resolute tone, its refusal of subtle nuance (which is not the same as crassness), reinforcing rather than belying the poet's huge disappointment.

Compared with 'Ariettes oubliées', the 'Paysages belges' are generally more outward-looking, as the title suggests. The themes of love, passivity and freedom are present in the poet's receptivity to the Belgian landscape, which, of course, is simultaneously his emotional landscape. In contrast to the 'Ariettes' which unfolded sensations and emotions, 'Paysages belges' tend to pile up sensations in a manner which resembles Rimbaud's poems of sensations, *Illuminations*. 'Voyance' includes pure receptivity to sensations. Nonetheless the poems are never exclusively verbal impressionism. They have their emotional depth.

'Walcourt' and 'Charleroi', like 'Bruxelles: Simples fresques', form diptychs which depict the pleasure and the pain of the exile in freedom. The mood of 'Walcourt' recalls that of 'Ariette' VI with its jolly conclusion to the brief and rapid description of the town through which Verlaine and Rimbaud walked on their way to Brussels in 1872, 'Quelles aubaines, / Bons juifs-errants!' (15-16), and which led him to compare the two friends with happy wanderers, whereas usually the wandering Jew is seen as a tragedy. On the other hand, the opening line of 'Charleroi', 'Dans l'herbe noire / Les Kobolds vont' echoes the eighth 'Ariette', 'Dans l'interminable / Ennui de la plaine' (1-2), just as the questioning, 'On sent donc quoi?' (13) echoes that of 'Ariette' V, 'Qu'est-ce que c'est que ce berceau soudain?' (7). In both instances despair is manifested in an unbridged gap between the senses, emotions and the faculty of understanding. In 'Le piano...' the poet's memory fails to recall the origin of the sensations; in 'Charleroi' the intellect fails to understand both the sensations and their source. The situation becomes worse still in the first of the 'Bruxelles' poems, 'Simples fresques': there is a near-failure of feeling. Like the fresco which fades with time, the poem deals with the passing of time, and so, of love *and* memory. The poem opens with detail and colour, 'La fuite est verdâtre et rose / Des collines et des rampes' (1-2). It closes with the moment when these details are 'apparences' only and are fast disappearing, '... tant s'effacent / Ces apparences d'automne' (9-10). All that remains of the original experience is a nameless bird, 'quelque oiseau faible chante. / Triste à peine' (8-9). The landscape, the experience is disappearing so fast that even the sadness is in doubt ('Triste à peine'). All that is left are the poet's 'langueurs', the essence of *not* feeling. The second 'fresque' presents a desperate wish for security, as if to halt the passing of time. A clear picture of a gravelled drive leads to a château surrounded by fields which, the poet had hoped, would be a haven for love, 'Oh! que notre amour / N'est-il là niché!' (17-18). However, the defiance of passing time and of failure of emotions is not guaranteed, for the achievement of emotional happiness is uncertain. The first 'Fresque' had questioned whether the experience had ever happened, so frail is memory. The desperate tone of 'Fresque' II conveys more of an unfulfilled wish than of certainty. The doubts and ambiguities posed in the ninth 'Ariette' persist.

'Chevaux de bois' is quite different in theme, tone and length from the other poems in 'Paysages belges'. Its loud, exciting evocation of a fairground scene anticipates the early twentieth-century simultaneity of Apollinaire's and Cendrars's poetry of urban life.[6] Juxtaposition of detail (5) and

[6] See G. Apollinaire, 'Zone', *Œuvres complètes* (Paris, Gallimard, Bibliothèque de la Pléiade, 1961), pp. 39-46; B. Cendrars, 'La Prose du

use of enumeration (1-2) are not confined to the external scene. The whirlpool of excitement is subjective too, 'C'est ravissant comme ça vous soûle' (13), and is willed into a state of being, 'Et dépêchez, chevaux de leur âme' (21). This active sensuality is the exact opposite of the sensual passivity so strongly sought in 'En sourdine' (*Fêtes galantes*). It clearly has connotations of personal intimacy, for the verse continues:

> Déjà voici que la nuit qui tombe
> Va réunir pigeon et colombe,
> Loin de la foire et loin de madame.   (22-24)

The arrival of night will once more unite the birds, the lovers, far from the noisy fair, far from *madame,* the archetypal wife and woman. The fair's excitement will be transmuted into the sexual ecstasy of the lovers.

The closing poem, 'Malines', constitutes a farewell to this cycle of poems, depicting as it does scenes glimpsed from a train. The poem is characterised by silence (11-12, 16) especially after the noisy activity of 'Chevaux de bois'. The train's carriages are rooms for intimate communication:

> Chaque wagon est un salon
> Où l'on cause bas et d'où l'on
> Aime à loisir cette nature
> Faite à souhait pour Fénelon.   (17-20)

And communication is but part of a more general harmony ('cette nature'). The allusion to Fénelon's doctrine of quietism completes the picture of silent harmony. This, an emotionally gentle close to the cycle, gives a note of completion contrasting with the section 'Aquarelles' which follows after the vicious interlude of 'Birds in the night' in which Verlaine criticises his young wife. The Belgian experience has been explored and understood: that of London will remain unresolved. In 'Aquarelles' the theme of freedom is treated

transsibérien' and 'Dix-neuf poèmes élastiques', *Poésies complètes* (Paris, Denoël, 1963), pp. 20-33, 51-80.

rather differently from the two previous sections. There is less consistent welcoming of freedom. In 'Green' and 'Spleen', love and passivity take the form of a full and open receptivity to the fleeting, essential moment in the emotional life. It is a bittersweet experience; the poet conveys his vulnerability in his request to his lover, ostensibly a woman (cf. 'mains blanches' (3), and 'jeune sein' (9), but it could equally be Rimbaud, for Verlaine refers to Rimbaud and himself as 'jeunes filles' in the fourth 'Ariette' (9)). Bearing gifts of supplication he asks for respite from 'la bonne tempête' of emotional turmoil, begging her/him to spare his heart: 'Ne le déchirez pas avec vos deux mains blanches' (3). The demand appears to be conditional on the loved one him/herself being in a state of relaxation, 'Et que je dorme un peu puisque vous reposez' (12). The use of the word 'puisque' recalls the 'logic' of 'A Clymène': 'Ainsi soit-il!' (*Fêtes galantes*) and so the unqualified emotional surrender to which the poet is liable. Moreover, the poet *anticipates* a moment of repose, in the future, just as he had imagined a place and time of security in the second of the 'Simples fresques'. There is no longer the freedom to enjoy the present moment, however troubled, as there was in 'Ariette' II. This situation is approached from another angle in the companion poem, 'Spleen'. Here too love and passivity entail fear of rejection, this time more openly, 'Je crains toujours – ce qu'est d'attendre! – / Quelque fuite atroce de vous' (7-8). And this time fear of the *moment* of rejection is the source of the poet's spleen, his lethargy, with the result that there is no freedom to savour the present moment. The vivid presentation of natural details (1-2) serves only to point up the poet's mood. Natural details obtrude and offend by the contrast between their freshness and the poet's depression, 'Le ciel était trop bleu, trop tendre, / La mer trop verte et l'air trop doux' (5-6). The loss of freedom is total, '... je suis las, ... de tout, fors de vous, hélas!' (10, 12). This situation recalls the Petrarchan dilemma in 'Dans la grotte' (*Fêtes galantes*), wherein the lover is unable to free himself from the captivity of love. The plaintive closing word 'Hélas!' takes on a far gloomier note than in the second 'Ariette' ('Je devine...'). There it denoted a bittersweet acceptance of necessary imperfection, but nonetheless an acceptance. In 'Spleen' the poet is slave to his emotions.

In contrast, the London-based 'Streets', I and II, present respectively a lighthearted farewell to the loved one and a vivid street scene in London. The poems' joyful energy conveys a momentary freedom, real or imagined, from the loved one, be it freedom from wanting Mathilde or from the depths of surrender to Rimbaud. It does not matter. What does matter is the mature understanding that happy memories are the positive reward of this freedom:

> Mais je trouve encore meilleur
> Le baiser de sa bouche en fleur,
> Depuis qu'elle est morte à mon cœur.   (10-12)

'Streets' II is an example of the clear, fresh vision that emotional freedom can bring, 'O la rivière dans la rue! / Fantastiquement apparue' (1-2). The poem, entirely a painted scene, and comparable in this to some of Rimbaud's *Illuminations,* is one of the few where the landscape (or, in this case, townscape) is free from any signs of reference to an inner landscape. This absence itself of course informs us of the poet's freedom from distress. Nothing interferes with his detailed and original observations of the world around him. Passivity can be this constructive receptivity to the external world. Here absence of love is seemingly the condition of freedom.

Together 'Child wife', 'A Poor Young Shepherd' and 'Beams' are about love. They enact, respectively, the process of leaving Mathilde, the early stages of love and the playful surrender to a new lover. The tone of these poems is markedly different from that of the other poems in the collection, with the exception of 'Birds in the night', although it is marginally prefigured in 'Streets'. The three poems have a Hugolian tone of declamation: love from a great distance and an impressive height. The child wife is told, 'Et vous n'aurez pas su la lumière et l'honneur / D'un amour brave et fort' (17-18). It is a stance of love, not the experience of love: 'Elle se retourna, doucement inquiète / De ne nous croire pas pleinement rassurés' ('Beams' 13-14). The emotions were raw at the beginning of this the third cycle ('Green', 'Spleen'), now they are hardened. The issue of freedom has been 'resolved' by evasion into externalised imagined scenes of parting, courtship and acquiescence to a new love, as it has into a poetic style which contrasts to the point of parody with the authentic Verlainian style.

In discussing *Fêtes galantes,* I referred to three themes, love, passivity and the mode of treatment, and suggested that the blending of these three in 'En sourdine' made that poem a significant link with *Romances sans paroles* (see above, p. 44). In *Romances sans paroles* the themes of love, passivity and freedom blend with the mode of treatment. In 'Ariette' II ('Je devine...') the unfolding presentation is appropriate to the theme of spiritual love; so too, and at the other extreme, is the chronological narrative of the popular song genre, to the unsubtle and strong emotions expressed in 'Birds in the night'. Running through the entire collection is a further layer. It is the pattern of emotional harmony and discord, a moving away from or towards one of these polarities. Some of the poems begin in a state of harmony and move towards discord. Thus 'Ariette' V ('Le piano que baise...') opens with a full evocation of finely nuanced sensations and progresses towards troubled questioning. 'Ariette' IX ('L'ombre des arbres') on the other hand remains harmonious in its consistent evocation of disappointment. Harmony does not necessarily imply happiness, although the harmonious joy in 'Walcourt' does involve both.

It is illuminating to consider the first and last three poems of *Romances sans paroles* in the light of this emotional pattern. As I have shown, the first three 'Ariettes' constitute a small cycle of poems in their own right, for they deal with the full range of Verlainian experience, sensual ecstasy, spiritual ideals and despair, all of which are expressed as an unfolding experiential process. The last three poems, 'Child wife', 'A Poor Young Shepherd' and 'Beams' also constitute an independent cycle of poems in their externalised stance of parting and loving anew. As such both 'cycles' offer vignettes of the Verlainian experience, both are harmonious in their tonal consistency. The first cycle is authentic, the second, an unconvincing pose. However, unlike 'Colloque sentimental' (*Fêtes galantes*), the lack of conviction in the second cycle does not cast a retrospective ambiguity over the whole collection. Instead it opens up questions concerning the diminution of the poems' quality, and so, the uneven quality of the poetry in the collection as a whole.

The key factor is the theme of freedom. If we consider the poems in their order of arrangement, which is not necessarily the order of composition, a picture emerges. In the first three 'Ariettes' freedom is of the essence of the experience, for the poems convey the poet's acceptance of the positive and negative aspects of the experience. The reassurance he seeks in 'C'est l'extase', the doubt itself, is part of the experience, as is the failed spiritual perfection in 'Je devine...' and the failure to understand the source of despair in 'Il pleure...' In the last three poems Verlaine adopts a *pose* of freedom, leaving a woman, beginning a new relationship; even the acquiescent love in 'Beams' is playful. Put another way, the first three 'Ariettes' do not question the ethical basis for this freedom, the situation is enjoyed and accepted for what it is; by the stage of the last three poems, the matter has been confronted and sidestepped.

So there is an unresolved conflict in the collection between emotional freedom and its ethical basis. This, the crucial and poignant discord, cuts across the collection and is the source of its tension. This discord concerns the issue of a *chosen* irresponsibility. In *Fêtes galantes* Verlaine justifies his amorality (see above, pp. 39-40), and 'Ariettes' IV and VII, 'Birds in the night' and 'Child wife' deal with the same matter, this time in the form of an irresponsibility not chosen, together with the attendant guilt and indictment of the beloved. These poems, circumstantially autobiographical, contrast with the other poems in the collection by dealing with specifically ethical matters. 'Ariettes' IV and VII present respectively the homosexual life with Rimbaud and the leaving of Mathilde, representing conventional heterosexual security; bohemianism versus social integration. In offering a justification for 'amorality', 'Ariette' IV develops the theme of 'A Clymène' (*Fêtes galantes*). In this 'Ariette' Verlaine's justification is an uncharacteristically assertive demand for forgiveness, 'Il faut ... nous pardonner les choses' (1). It is obviously possible to read this line as referring to some undisclosed violation of an unstated code. Indeed the vagueness is the very condition to which he refers; homosexual love was inadmissible in nineteenth-century France and, as Oscar Wilde put it, 'dared not speak its name'. There is possibly a sense of sin in the choice of the word 'pardonner', given Verlaine's subsequent reconversion to Catholicism during his imprisonment in Mons prison after the shooting incident, and in view of the fact that he was given the maximum sentence of two years' hard labour, less for shooting at Rimbaud than for practising sodomy with a minor. In 'Ariette' IV, Verlaine insists on a life of freedom which, given the reference to the poets as 'filles' (9), is doubtless passive in the sense of rejecting coventional notions of masculinity. Depending on one's point of view, the seventh 'Ariette' ('O triste...') captures, as I have suggested, the paradox of being separated without being separate; equally it could convey the self-pity of a man who cannot have his cake and eat it.

'Birds in the night' evokes a similarly ambiguous response. It is by far the longest poem in the collection, narrating the poet's emotional life with a woman from the beginning of the relationship to a parting which clearly does not constitute the end of the relationship. The overt theme of the poem is the poet's forgiveness of the woman. I do not doubt the sincerity of this, given Verlaine's collections of poems such as *La Bonne Chanson* and *Sagesse*. I find the criterion of sincerity difficult with respect to poetry and prefer to leave it aside as being ultimately unuseful for assessing the merits of a poem. In the final analysis the poem should stand on its own. Letting 'Birds in the night' do just that, I find it has little aesthetic merit, with its banal verse form, rhyme scheme and relentless list of undoubtedly powerful but nonetheless crassly expressed emotions. And indeed I find that in the place of any such merit the emotional content intrudes itself. This is the point: the poem refuses any response of the order which we are accustomed to give to most of the poems in the collection. Instead it presents itself with a tone of appalling self-pity and cowardly self-justification. The same is true of 'Child wife' which begins, 'Vous n'avez rien compris à ma simplicité'. As with 'Birds in the night', the fact that Verlaine obviously believes such assertions is ultimately irrelevant. For the overt theme of self-pity and cruel criticism of Mathilde's understandably annoying childish behaviour is contradicted by a tone of quite staggering indictment of the young wife. The poem ends with a grandiose and ludicrous Hugolian utterance indicating all that the young wife has missed through her failure to understand her husband. Presumably the Hugolian echoes are further justification for the criticism of the wife. Hugo's life is doubtless the ideal to which all poets *and* wives should aspire. Adèle Hugo had, after all, 'understood' *her* husband's infidelities.

These four poems, autobiographical, and expressing the tension between freedom and security, are Verlaine's 'Saison en enfer'. *Fêtes galantes* had presented an ethos of freedom from responsibility in the transposition to the imaginary *fête galante* world. In *Romances sans paroles* the matter is focused into a choice between a free, 'immoral' life with Rimbaud or a life of conventional security with Mathilde. Verlaine seems to choose neither; or rather he *refuses to choose*. In the last analysis, the direction chosen is irrelevant; what matters is the choice between responsibility and amorality. Verlaine does not even choose to be amoral; this is the ultimate, and damaging, irresponsibility. His change of lifestyle with Rimbaud has hardly proved to be the free amoral world imagined in *Fêtes galantes*. The promise of the *fête galante* world has not been realised. The poet is faced instead with the consequences of his chronic refusal to choose; they are aesthetic as well as ethical consequences.

The quality of the poetry in *Romances sans paroles* is patchy compared with that of *Fêtes galantes*. Verlaine's best art is written under the successfully self-deceiving illusion of acceptance that love is passive irresponsibility. Moreover, in these poems, particularly the 'Ariettes', the positive and negative dimensions of the situation are maturely explored. However, in the poems where no such illusions are created, and where a more recognisably personal matter intrudes, Verlaine simply misses the essence of the moment in question. So, it is when he deals with the serious source of his delicious irresponsibility and which he ultimately evades by blaming Mathilde for everything, that the poetry borders on the banal. In such poems Verlaine misses the core of the emotion: 'Tout le reste est littérature'. This, the last line from 'Art poétique', Verlaine's own criticism of 'unmusical' poetry, judges, sadly, its own author. With Verlaine's critique in mind, together with his own dramatic lapses from this ideal of musicality, it is time to turn our attention to the large question of music in *Fêtes galantes* and *Romances sans paroles,* beginning with Verlaine's art of versification.

3

'De la Musique avant toute chose'

T H I S frequently quoted line from Verlaine's 'Art poétique' sums up his ideas concerning the kind of poetry he considered he was writing. The question is, what does he mean by such a vague term? In the absence of anything more definite, apart, of course, from Verlaine's 'recipes' in the poem for *achieving* musical poetry, I hope, in this chapter, to offer several possible answers. Overall, I think we can usefully consider the term 'Musique' in two distinct ways, the literal and the metaphorical, that is, Verlaine's art of versification and a poetry which is non-intellectual and moving as far as is possible towards a poetry of disembodied sensations. These distinctions share the premise of poetry's power to generate feelings through sounds and rhythms as well as through verbal suggestion.

As with the thematic content of the collections, Verlaine's poetic art rests on a paradox, a precise exploitation and extension of the rules of versification: 'j'ai élargi la discipline du vers et cela est bon; mais je ne l'ai pas supprimée' (*22,* p. 69), as Verlaine says. French verse is characterised by its discipline, for instance the rule of alternating feminine and masculine rhymes. It is noted too for its versatility. Far from being rigid, such discipline permits and indeed defines innovation. Verlaine's poetic art in *Fêtes galantes* and *Romances sans paroles* continues the Parnassian and more especially the Baudelarian practice of extending the range of expressive possibilities available to French verse. In particular he develops what Baudelaire terms a 'sorcellerie évocatoire', a poetry of suggestion. In 'Art poétique' Verlaine variously refers to this notion as 'l'Indécis' (8), 'la Nuance' (13) and 'la Musique'

(1). I want to stress that the poem's celebrated line, 'Où l'Indécis au Précis se joint' (8) is not a contradiction, for, as Baudelaire pointed out, authentic 'sorcellerie' can only result from craftsmanship: 'Manier savamment une langue, c'est pratiquer une espèce de sorcellerie évocatoire' (*10*, vol. II, p. 118). In *Romances sans paroles* particularly, Verlaine has achieved an exact bending and extending of the rules. 'Précis' too, embraces the concept of the fleeting moment which this art captures with a deadly accuracy. Verlaine obviously treated versification with what we might term a respectful disrespect. For him the poetic line is 'la bonne aventure', 'la chose envolée' ('Art poétique', 30, 33), a source of other, unknown regions of the heart and senses, 'Vers d'autres cieux à d'autres amours' (32).

In *Fêtes galantes* and *Romances sans paroles* Verlaine shifts the emphasis from 'correct' rhyming[7] to an exploration and exploitation of the sensuous, rich sounds inherent in rhyme endings. Not surprisingly this is more the case with *Romance sans paroles* given that collection's more direct concern with various and varying states of passivity. In *Fêtes galantes,* on the other hand, rhyme schemes range from the formal and unobtrusive to the mildly expressive. The regular *abab* scheme of 'En patinant' blends with the regular stanza form and does not detract from the poem's narrative. In contrast the rich rhyming pattern throughout 'A Clymène, the sounds of which occur more frequently because of the short line lengths, creates a dense sound resonance echoing the surrender of the self to sensations which the poem evokes.

Of particular note in *Fêtes galantes* is Verlaine's use of the *b* rhymes in poems of three-line stanzas. For example 'Pantomime', 'Fantoches', 'Cythère' and 'Les Indolents' break the norm of the single-rhymed triplet, i.e. *aaa,* which qualifies it as a stanza, and establish a new rhyme scheme

---

[7] For a comprehensive study of French versification, the reader is referred to M. Grammont, *Le Vers français* (Paris, Delagrave, 1964), L. E. Kastner, *A History of French Versification* (Oxford, Clarendon Press, 1903), R. Lewis, *On Reading French Verse* (Oxford, Clarendon Press, 1982), C. Scott, *French Verse-Art: a study* (Cambridge University Press, 1980), and *The Riches of Rhyme: Studies in French Verse* (Oxford, Clarendon Press, 1988).

commensurate with the alternative reality of the *fête galante* world. In 'Cythère' the *b* rhyme is maintained and its position is reversed halfway through the poem (*aab, ccb, bdd, bee*). This creates a mirror-like effect suggestive of a further independent world, an impossible land free from responsibility. So too with 'Les Indolents' where the rhyme scheme is actually expanded with the addition of g and h rhymes (*aab, ccb, dde, ffe, ggb, hhb*). The addition literally expands the idealised world of Cythera, explores its amorality, while the insistent and different *e* rhyme draws attention to its semantics, 'ensemble' 'semble' (9, 12); the ambiguous relationship between the illusion of harmony and reality, the essence of the *fête galante* world. With the repositioning of the *b* rhyme at the end of the poem, it assumes a dominant sound, as if all is moving in the poem towards that second rhyme, anxious to consolidate and keep intact the hard-won land of exquisite sensation.

'Mandoline' and 'En sourdine' demonstrate Verlaine's use of masculine and feminine rhymes. 'Mandoline' is composed entirely of feminine rhymes. The unpronounced final syllable of the feminine rhyme leaves an openness of sound, a faint echo. Cumulatively across the poem's sixteen lines the feminine rhymes, enhanced by a coincidence of rhyme and grammatical gender, create a gentle, insistent harmony. The open [a] sound of the rhymes at the end of the poem 'jase', 'extase' (13, 15), echoes the opening rhyme 'sérénades', 'fades' (1, 3). The expected harmony appears to be confirmed by the semantics of 'extase' only to be shattered by that of its rhyme 'jase', itself the only verb in the rhyme endings. This element of discord is all the more perturbing for its apparent blending with the rhyme scheme; a discreet tension between sound and semantics quietly asserts itself. On the other hand the exclusively masculine rhyme in 'En sourdine', with its characteristic of closed finality, paradoxically conveys the poet's purposeful and determined progress into a world free from the constraints of the intellect. The rigidity of the rhyme hints too at certain failure, further underlined by the future tense 'Voix de notre désespoir, / Le rossignol chantera' (19-20).

Verlaine is known particularly for his use of a great variety of line lengths in these collections, especially the *vers impair,* a line with an uneven number of syllables. In *Romances sans paroles* Verlaine exploits the potential of using an uneven number of syllables, a practice for whose reintroduction into French poetry he is mainly responsible. The heptasyllabic (seven syllable) line, the one most usually employed by him, was commonly used by medieval lyric poets. Verlaine did, after all, give his poems the title *Romances sans paroles.* With the use of the heptasyllable in *Romances sans paroles,* Verlaine extends this tradition of the intimate lyrical song. The line can convey a vague sense of the disturbing (as already in *Fêtes galantes,* 'En sourdine'), the ambiguous emotion of the first 'Simples fresques' in *Romances sans paroles,* or the considerably less ambiguous sensuality of the first 'Ariette', 'C'est l'extase...' Yet in so far as the line is not completed aurally and rhythmically into eight syllables, it leaves open infinite suggestive possibilities, emotional and aural resonances. The semantic and monosyllabic certainty of 'C'est' only points, by contrast, the exquisite and quite probably indescribable sensations conveyed in the coupling of the two trisyllabic words 'extase langoureuse'. And while the open feminine ending hints at a further 'completing' syllable, not because of any absolute rule versification, but because of French verse habits which have tended to use eight, ten or twelve syllable lines, in this instance, there is no sense of needing to 'complete'. On the contrary, to add the eighth syllable would be to remove the significance of the unuttered.

In this practice of what Martino calls 'cette façon de démolir intérieurement le rythme du vers' (*25,* p. 173), Verlaine is but a short step from his extensive use of the *coupe* which effectively overthrows conventional pauses in creating a new dimension of rhythmic accentuation which conveys an emotional dynamic. Not surprisingly this art is at its most accomplished in the 'Ariettes oubliées', notably those written in the *vers impair* where the 'extra' syllable readily lends itself to a resonant displacement of the stress, as in 'Ariette' I, 'la mienne, dis, et la tienne' (16). The *coupe* 'dis, / et la tienne' breaks the line dramatically. The pause is long and the halting rhythm conveys more poignantly the poet's anxiety. With more stresses the line takes longer to read. These rhythms, I believe, 'tell' of emotional changes independently of the semantic 'meaning' of the poem.

Sound patterns are a vital source of the poems' subtle shifts in emotional tone. *Fêtes galantes* and *Romances sans paroles* demonstrate Verlaine's development of the use of sound patterns into a sophisticated art. Onomatopœia, alliteration and assonance[8] barely account for this aspect of Verlaine's art, in spite of his preference for the onomatopœic words 'murmure' and 'sangloter' and the obvious repetition of the assonantal [u] in 'Chevaux de bois' to convey the poem's no less obvious frenetic sexuality. Together sound patterns and rhythm constitute a major source of what Verlaine terms in 'Art poétique' the poem's 'Nuance' (13), and which, for him 'fiance / Le rêve au rêve et la flûte au cor!' (15-16). That is, significantly linked *disparate* sounds convey 'le rêve', and as such help make of the poetic line 'la chose envolée' (30), 'la bonne aventure' (33) into new realms of experience, the fleeting moment, emotional, sensual, and, at times, spiritual. The word and experience are united. In 'Mandoline' Verlaine uses the [u] sound in the word 'Tourbillonnent' (13) in quite a different way from 'Chevaux de bois'. In 'Mandoline' the harmonious mingling of dancer and dance, of self and sensations, rhythm especially, reaches its fulfilment in this word, placed as it is as the head word of the final verse. As the *rejet* of the *enjambement* from the previous verse, the delay of the slight pause between the verses makes the rhythmic stress on this word all the stronger. The symmetry of the word's four syllables dominates the seven-syllable line. This straightforwardness is matched by the simple onomatopœic quality of the word, itself a commentary on the ease of the *fête galante* characters' uniting.

In a number of poems Verlaine uses the device of the *rime en écho,* an internal repeated rhyme, in such a way that the sound patterns resulting are not so much alliterative or assonantal as a sound modulation appropriate to the poetic

---

[8] For further details, see M. Grammont, *Le Vers français* (Paris, Delagrave, 1964), pp. 62-64, 196-200, and C. Scott, 'Word Sound' in *French Verse-Art: a study* (Cambridge University Press, 1980), pp. 94-103.

theme. 'Clair de lune' has two *rimes en écho.* The first straddles two verses 'Et leur chanson se mêle au *clair* de *lune,* / Au calme *clair* de *lune* triste et beau' (8-9). This use of *rime en écho* to repeat and modulate sounds, which focuses the reader's attention on the adjectives 'calme', 'triste' and 'beau', prefigures that in the final two lines, 'Et sangloter d'extase *les jets d'eau, / Les* grands *jets d'eau* sveltes parmi les marbres' (11-12). As is usual with this kind of repetition, our attention is first drawn to the semantics of the words which surround the repeated words, 'sangloter', 'd'extase', 'grands', 'sveltes'. Rendered stronger by the sexual symbolism, these words are extraordinarily strong and sensual ones to use of nature, albeit an artificial eighteenth-century nature, and as such tell us of the transfiguring power of the moonlight and so of the successful move into the 'paysage choisi' of the poet's soul.

Similarly Verlaine uses assonance and alliteration, on a broad scale, across a poem to create a background sound which signifies an emotional tone, as in the third verse of 'Mandoline' where the alliteration of [l] produces a gentle lulling sound 'realised' in the words 'l'extase' (13), 'lune' (14) and 'mandoline' (15), and in the fourth verse, the verse of near-fulfilled ecstasy. This, together with the assonantal [œ] which dominates the third verse, and which is echoed in the rhyme 'queues' (10) and 'bleues' (12), contributes to the, for once, easy process of harmony which the poem evokes.

But Verlaine's art of the resonating modulated sound is at its most subtle in the 'Ariettes oubliées'. In the first verse of 'Ariette' V, 'Le piano...', which evokes infinite and ever-changing subtleties of lingering sound and perfume, Verlaine uses sound patterns in both pairs and triplets to create highly 'local' sound modifications which nonetheless resonate across the poem as lingering sensations in themselves. This is true of the fifth and sixth lines, 'Rôde discret, épeuré quasiment, / Par le boudoir longtemps parfumé d'Elle'. The alternation of voiced and voiceless consonants [d, d, k, p, k, p, b, d, t, p, d] evokes the ebb and flow of the ever-distant sensations. The predominant plosives [p, b] and the nasals in the remainder of the two lines evoke the eerie, taunting and intangible sensations. The pattern of plosives embracing nasals, 'épeuré quasiment / Par' [p-ã-p] is repeated and expanded in 'boudoir longtemps parfumé [b-ã-p]. Quite literally the empty, echoing nasal drone accords with its meaning, 'longtemps'. The echo is drawn out, fading and impenetrable. The effect is enhanced in the tenth line where Verlaine uses the triplet of words with the same sound, 'fin refrain incertain'. The relatively close repetition of the nasal [ɛ̃] sound which is arranged in the pattern of a mirror image, captures the essence of the nightmarish situation, the insistence of memory wanting to know the origins of the ever-fading sensations.

In the final line of 'Art poétique', 'Et tout le reste est littérature', Verlaine draws a distinction between his poetry of nuanced suggestiveness and a poetry of more direct utterance, descriptive, narrative, intellectual even. In this sense Verlaine appears to be using the word 'Musique' as a metaphor.

Many poets and musicians of the mid- and late nineteenth century concerned themselves with the connections between poetry and music. Mallarmé considered poetry superior to music, '[C'est) de l'intellectuelle parole à son apogée que doit avec plénitude et évidence, résulter, en tant que l'ensemble des rapports existant dans tout, la Musique' (*24*, p. 368). The poetic word, in its profoundest sense, is sacred, with its power to create meaning, to assume the supreme poetic task of expressing the inexpressible. Elsewhere Mallarmé uses the term 'music' to indicate a poetry able to capture an essence: 'c'est bien le pur de nous-mêmes par nous porté' (*24*, p. 334). In fact 'music' had as many definitions as the people using it. Yet one factor unites these definitions, namely the idea that music concerns the expression of some kind of essence, the poet's particular ideal. In his philosophical work, *The World as Will and Idea* (1819), Schopenhauer enlists music's capacity for direct expression in his protest against rational ideals, thereby giving a more abstract account of the importance held by music in the intellectual and aesthetic climate in which Verlaine was writing:

> Music is thus by no means like the other arts the copy of the Ideas, but the *copy of the will itself,* whose objectivity the Ideas

are. This is why the effect of music is so much more powerful
and penetrating than that of the other arts, for they speak only
of shadows, but it speaks of the thing itself.[9]

Whereas Baudelaire's ideal was a harmonious world tran-
scending the conflict between the moral and the physical,
Mallarmé's a region of pure thought and Rimbaud's a vision
uncontaminated by Western civilisation, Verlaine's ideal in
Romances sans paroles is on a less grandiose scale, and its
spiritual quality of a rather different order. This is a search
for the experience of sensations and emotions for and in
themselves, devoid of logical context and event. Some of
course would not consider this quest as a 'spiritual' ideal,
preferring the more recognisable and familiar spirituality of
Verlaine's return to Catholicism in *Sagesse*. Verlaine's quest
for these states, as indeed for a fresh and appropriate poetic
expression of them, properly constitutes the poems' spirituality and, as such, is an important source of the poems'
'musicality'.

In a letter of May 1873 to Lepelletier, Verlaine outlines a
poetry he is still aiming for:

> Je caresse l'idée de faire ... un livre de poèmes ... d'où
> *l'homme* sera complètement banni. Des paysages, des choses,
> malice des choses, bonté, etc., etc., des choses ... Ça sera très
> musical, sans puérilités à la Poë ... et aussi pittoresque que
> possible ... c'est peut-être une idée chouette que j'ai là. (*8*, vol.
> I, pp. 98-99)

His awareness of the dangers of 'sound effects' leads him to
speculate on the possibility of a poetry of landscapes and
near-disembodied sensations, a poetry for which the term
'musical' is a metaphor, imprecise though it be. In this
respect the 'music' in *Fêtes galantes* and *Romances sans
paroles* lies both in the various and varying states of passivity

[9] A. Schopenhauer, *The World as Will and Idea,* translated by R. B.
Haldane and J. Kemp (1883), (London, Routledge and Kegan Paul, 1957),
p. 333.

which Verlaine evokes and the methods he employs to do this.

The changing status of the pictorial in the collections charts the poems' progress to the Verlainian essence of these states of passivity. This evolution redefines 'le pittoresque' from a fairly crude symbolism in *Fêtes galantes,* through unambiguous landscapes to the infinitely nuanced and suggestive 'Aquarelles', the pictorial as embodiment of sensations and emotions independent of a particular individual; an impersonal poetry. It seems to me that in 'Ariettes oubliées' Verlaine achieves instances of supreme quality. This authentic and original fusion of inner and outer worlds is perhaps most successful in the eighth 'Ariette'. The desolate scene *is* simultaneously the poet's desolate soul. The two cannot be 'read' separately, as is possible with the *fête galante* pictures. The scene tells poignantly and fully of the poet's imprisoned and emotionally barren state, and vice versa. 'Ennui' is after all as much a physical as an emotional condition. Even so, the first and second 'Ariettes', sensations and emotions without a scene, are no less convincing. The first 'Ariette': 'C'est l'extase...' is nothing but the evocation of sensations *experienced* in change as distinct from sensations *observed* in change such as we find in *Fêtes galantes.* These 'scenes' in the 'Ariettes' invite a more involved response from the reader than do the pictures of *Fêtes galantes,* whose significance lies precisely in their distance from the reader. In the 'Ariettes', disembodied sensations have been re-embodied with the pictorial. It is doubtless in this area that the example of Rimbaud is most evident.

The move to the new pictorial modes signalled by the titles, 'Paysages', 'Fresques' and 'Aquarelles', indicates an evolution from landscapes to watercolour, washes of colour to which the medium of water gives full visual resonance, and so demands a greater involvement of the reader's imagination. This helps to make less personal and more universal those sensations and emotions already relatively disembodied in the 'Ariettes'. Even so I would argue that the notion is taken to its limits, perhaps too far. The result is some weakening, a flattening of impact. What do we respond to

– the picture or the emotional overtones – as in, for instance, the second of the 'Simples fresques', 'L'allée est sans fin / Sous le ciel, divin / D'être pâle ainsi' (1-3)? The relationship of picture to emotion is not always apparent. Yet the pictures are Verlaine's own, not Watteau's. Nonetheless Verlaine's most authentic pictures remain most of the 'Ariettes', with their direct expression of sensual and emotional experience through rhythm and sound and where no over-intrusive pictorial dimension puts an obstacle between the feeling self and poetic expression. [10]

It is of course, entirely relevant that the later, more pictorial poems are, generally, more concerned with pain than with pleasure and may demand the strongly pictorial as some kind of safeguard, as in the *Fêtes galantes*. But a significant number of the 'Ariettes' also express deep pain, and here Verlaine's symbolist impressionism is at its most 'musical', evoking states of being, not of doing, and using, with tact, the pictorial to embody sensations and emotions which otherwise risk being given an unhelpfully vague expression. [11]

As a result there is no shortage of *pictures* in the collections, but generally, these are not *images*. The power of imagery has been replaced by that of sound and rhythmic textures. These textures are literally the poems' presentation of sensations and so of feelings. Inspiration and expression derive from the same source. The reversed sound and pattern of [R d d s k R] in line 2 of the fifth 'Ariette', 'rôde discret' is heightened by the inverted [s] and [k] sounds and suggests, by its near-palindromic mirroring of sounds, the sense of imprisonment. The semantics confirm this. The extent that sounds

[10] For a study of Verlaine's art of impressionism the reader is referred to O. Nadal, 'L'Impressionisme verlainien' *Mercure de France,* May 1952, pp. 59-72; M. Got, '"Art Poétique": Verlaine et la technique impressionniste', *Table Ronde,* vol. 159, March 1961, pp. 128-36; Russell S. King, 'Verlaine's verbal sensations', *Studies in Philology,* vol. LXII, 1975, pp. 226-36; and N. Ruwet, 'Mystique et vision chez Verlaine' in *Langue française,* vol. 49, 1981, pp. 92-112 for a highly detailed analysis of 'Walcourt' (*Romances sans paroles*) and of *Sagesse,* III, vi.

[11] For an opposite view I refer the reader to *37.* Stephan suggests that the impressionist art of the poem 'Walcourt' tells us of the poet's joy.

and rhythms signify in this manner means that they *are* musical, not *like* music.

Obviously sound and rhythm help make of the poetry of *Fêtes galantes* and *Romances sans paroles* a form of 'sensationnisme', a poetry appealing predominantly to the senses. Already in *Fêtes galantes* the poet's surrender to his loved one in 'A Clymène' is 'justified' by the effect she has upon his senses. Often the senses are intermingled with, for example, smell and sight: 'l'arôme insigne / De ta pâleur de cygne' (9-10). This process is known as synaesthesia and Baudelaire's poetry is most directly influential on Verlaine in this respect. Indeed, Baudelaire's sonnet 'Correspondances' is devoted to the concept of synaesthesia and its spiritual dimensions (*10,* vol. I, p. 11). One of the hallmarks of Verlaine's poetry is this direct appeal to the reader's *synaesthetic imagination,* the capacity to *imagine* through his or her senses. 'C'est l'extase...', the first 'Ariette', contains, at the very least, the sensations of intensity and relaxation, rapid and slow movement, sound and silence.

In a general sense, synaesthesia, along with onomatopœia and rhythm, of which it is a part, is one of the main features of the poems and a source of their suggestiveness. The pictorial aspect of synaesthesia constitutes a crucial element of the entire synaesthetic process, for synaesthesia operates on the principle of association. With the pictorial, association has been intensified firstly into equivalence, 'Vôtre âme est un paysage choisi' ('Clair de lune', 1) and thereafter, into symbol.

Association is the essence, and I want at this point to propose a clearer relationship between two terms I have deliberately used in a looser connection: sensations and emotions. In varying degrees, Verlaine's evocation of sensations *suggests* emotional states, and in some way may symbolise them. The overt eroticism of 'Les Coquillages' suggests a deep isolation; the decidedly subtler sensations of smell and hearing in the fifth 'Ariette' tell of a precarious emotional balance. Certainly senses are as much the source of the emotions as the emotions are of the senses. The close relationship between emotions and the senses is at the heart of Verlainian impressionist symbolism.

Apart from the overall visual sense, touch is the predominant sense in these collections, whereas in Baudelaire's poetry it is the sense of smell. I imply no value judgement and simply wish to observe that in Verlaine's poetry the tactile sense can and does override those senses, usually more powerful, if only because more familiar, of sight and smell. It is perhaps worth pointing out too that the sense of touch has more scope for the associative processes of the synaesthetic *imagination,* as distinct from more physical sense associations. Thus movement and touch combine in 'Lors sa fille, ... / Sous la charmille, ... / Se glisse, demi-nue' ('Fantoches', 7-9). Clothes seem to have an autonomous existence with their sumptuousness, 'Leurs courtes vestes de soie, / Leurs longues robes à queues' ('Mandoline', 9-10). Touch of course is the most intimate sense of all: 'C'est tous les frissons des bois / Parmi l'étreinte des brises' ('Ariette', I, 3-4).

The sense of hearing plays a distinctively consistent role. In *Fêtes galantes* references to music and musicians invariably herald a transition to a personal reverie: music is the mediator for an ideal world. Accordingly the sense of hearing signals a process of transformation from outer to inner world, being as it is essentially musical: 'sangloter d'extase' ('Clair de lune', 11), 'Le rossignol chantera' ('En sourdine', 20). In the 'Ariettes', sound evokes intimacy in the first, idealism in the second. In this latter the sense of sound is combined with a highly refined synaesthetic process which hovers tantalisingly between a physical and spiritual world, bringing with it fresh synaesthetic perceptions.

This associative unfolding synaesthetic process constitutes an important element of the poems' thematic structure. Senses evoke emotions, and shifting emotional states, as we have seen, are predominantly the poems' themes. This interconnection of synaesthesia and thematic structure is the source of its self-referring quality. Such an art, on a small as well as on a large scale, is an art of presentation; of unfolding experience, not of representation or description. In particular it conforms to a major notion underlying Pater's well-known assertion, 'All art constantly aspires to the condition of music'. [12] Such poetry is often referred to as 'pure poetry', an abstract poetry in the sense that it has no other subject but itself. Mossop's reference to T. S. Eliot's understanding of this term is illuminating: 'Mr Eliot explains the idea of pure poetry in terms of a tendency to regard the subject of the poem, not as an end in itself, but as a means to the end which is the poem' (*27,* p. 5).

Verlaine's symbolist impressionism evokes an autonomous, alternative world. This happens to be a statedly amoral world, free from responsibility, be it the ritual of 'L'Allée', or the anxious, doubting questions in the first 'Ariette'. But the fourth 'Ariette' quite openly demands such an existence: 'Il faut, voyez-vous, nous pardonner les choses' (1). Amorality is both a correlative of, and a condition for, Verlaine's world of passivity and exquisite sensations. His creation of this autonomous amoral world through the art of symbolist impressionism can equally be regarded as a form of pure poetry, with the minimum of representational meaning. Mossop puts the matter clearly: 'abstraction, ... the withdrawal or distance of the content of the pure poem from the events and situations of everyday life ... this causes an unusually high degree of fusion between subjective and objective elements in the poem' (*28,* pp. 92-93). Edmund Wilson makes much the same point, and from an interesting angle, in his discussion of symbolist poetry which, he claims, 'suggest[s] imaginary worlds made up of elements abstracted from our experience of the real world and revealing relationships which we acknowledge to be valid within those fields of experience'. [13] The worlds of *Fêtes galantes* and *Romances sans paroles* exemplify these definitions with their essentially uncomplicated theme, an emotion, and one which permits multivalent associations.

The tension between harmony and discord, the move to resolve opposites, constitute the structure of many of the

---

[12] W. Pater, 'The School of Giorgione' in *The Renaissance* (London, Fontana, 1961), p. 129.

[13] E. Wilson, *Axel's Castle* (London, Fontana, 1976), p. 234.

poems. Verlaine's poems share this feature with music to a high degree; they do not borrow it from music. Indeed the technique of the *vers impair* has this tension built into it. Most of the poems seek to resolve a particular conflict, to harmonise some discord, and quite often fail to do so. The links with the Verlainian emotional dilemma are obvious enough. In 'L'Allée' the harmonious picture of the *fête galante* woman becomes increasingly disturbed by the uncomfortable impossibility of ever knowing the woman more intimately, 'la bouche / Incarnadine, grasse et divine d'orgueil / Inconscient' (11-13). Significantly enough, a harmonious resolution is the outcome of 'A Clymène' with the poem's spurious liturgy, the delicious surrender to love, 'Ainsi soit-il!' (20). This emotional and sensuous surrender is hardly difficult; the fight against it seems not to have been particularly strong, any more than it was for Oscar Wilde who shares Verlaine's morally roguish tone; 'I couldn't help it. I can resist anything but temptation'.[14]

The poems' progress towards a degree of harmonising of opposites is the main source of their distinctive time-scale. Poetry and music are distinguished from painting and sculpture by the dimension of time. Lessing makes the point eloquently: 'The painter employs figures and colours in *space,* the poet articulates sounds in time'.[15] The poem's move to harmonising opposites, its principal time-scale, is overlaid in some cases by other time-scales. Those of the 'Ariettes' are undoubtedly the most interesting. The sensations evoked in most of these poems are simultaneously those of one specific moment and of eternity, of no time at all; the particular and the universal. This is overlaid by the time it takes us to read the poem on the page. Time is an emotional and physical reality. The time-scale of the poems *is* the experience evoked. This strongly experiential aspect of the poems (evoking recognisable sensations and emotions) is

[14] O. Wilde, 'Lady Windermere's Fan', Act I, *Plays* (London, Penguin, 1975), p. 44.
[15] G. E. Lessing, *Laocoon,* translation and notes by R. Phillimore (London, Routledge, 1910), p. 44.

the essence of Verlaine's poetry of presentation. The poems share with music the power of sensuous and emotional communication.

Debussy's and Fauré's settings of Verlaine's poems respond to the music of the poetry as something beyond even the sensuous sounds and rhythms and the journey into an imaginative world, which characterise their settings of Baudelaire. This 'something' is, I believe, concerned with the Verlainian art of conveying the *process* of subtly changing sensibility, the art of tensions and relaxations, so that, in common with music, the poetry combines emotional and sensuous power with the dimension of time. The *emotional* effect of a glimpsed perfection, in 'En sourdine', counterpointed by a failure which poignantly underlines that perfection, this effect is comparable to hearing a cadence which is not resolved or completed; we 'hear' with our inner ear what the completed cadence will be. And yet it does not happen; a moment of mingled pain and pleasure.

The response to this poem's emotional line characterises Debussy's and Fauré's settings of a number of Verlaine's poems. In general, Debussy's settings tend to enhance the music of the poems both as emotional meaning and as patterns of rhythm and sound. His setting of 'En sourdine' (from the first series of *Fêtes galantes,* 1891), is typical of this kind of response. For instance the vocal line in the setting of the first verse is more like a recitative than a melody. The accompaniment, a succession of rootless chords, and slow harmonies, evokes the deliberately blurred and unchanging scene. In the third verse, the verse of definite mood change, the accompaniment takes over from the voice and becomes its own expression, echoing the sensuous passivity which the poet seeks in this verse. Triplets envelop the voice in chromatic harmonies as it sings 'Ferme tes yeux à demi' which replace the earlier simpler pentatonic scale, a far richer sound conveying fulfilment. This process of envelopment is reversed across the setting as a whole. The last syllable of 'extasiés', set on D sharp, is echoed in the final syllable of the last word 'chantera', also set on D sharp, an octave lower and twice as long. The melodic arabesque sweeps downwards and the note of resolution which is implicit in the D sharp is denied by the accompaniment which closes on an unresolved chord of G sharp. Perfection is not achieved. This tension between resolution and discord is emphasised further by dramatic variations in the rhythmic pattern.

Unlike Debussy, Fauré puts the musical before the verbal element in his setting, and focuses less on the more evident emotional and sonorous dimensions of the poem than on giving rhythmic and sonorous expression to its further possible and less evident meanings. His setting of this poem, on the other hand, consistently uses repeated semiquaver arpeggios, that is, broken chords, which give the song a formal musical unity. He straightforwardly matches syllables with note values in the opening line: 'Calmes' is spread over five crotchets, while 'dans le demi-jour' has just three. This simple matching paradoxically gives greater scope to the rich resonances of the simple key change. The first syllable of 'Pénétrons' for instance, is set on a raised fourth, and this slight sound change signifies profoundly with its introduction of a chromatic vagueness, underlining the furthest stage of merging sensations and nature which the word 'Pénétrons' invites. Unlike Debussy too, Fauré sets the final syllable of 'extasiés' on low G sharp, the final note of a descending melodic line, marked *diminuendo,* fading away. It is, then, a muted ecstasy which prefigures by sound, the 'failure' implied in the poem's closing line. The sound suggests something which the word 'extasiés' denies. Similarly the accompaniment to 'Ferme tes yeux', in a minor key, blends with the vocal line. It does not take it over, as if to suggest to some a degree of self-control, self-awareness, irony even, to others a total fusion of the individual with nature.

4

Conclusion

> A little sincerity is a dangerous thing, and a great deal of it is absolutely fatal.
>
> (O. Wilde, *The Critic as Artist)*

FÊTES galantes and *Romances sans paroles* offer a profoundly serious exploration of passion and amorality. Verlaine's refusal of responsibility in his own life is expressed, in his art, in the evocation and exploration of various states and degrees of exquisite passivity. It is, ultimately, a world no more attainable than Baudelaire's *vie antérieure,* Mallarmé's *absolu* or that pure world sought by Rimbaud's *voyance* in, among other poems, 'Le Bateau ivre' and the *Illuminations.* Rimbaud's admission of this 'failure', acutely and bitterly recorded in *Une Saison en enfer* (1873), has no comparable equivalent in Verlaine's work. Instead the reader is faced, simply, with different and highly distinctive *kinds* of Verlainian poetry; a poetry of subtle feeling and a poetry of embarrassing sentimentality, usually of a confessional nature presenting the triumph of God over human sensuality, as in his poem 'Crimen amoris' (*Jadis et naguère,* 1885), or purely hedonistic poems such as *Femmes* (1890). Both kinds of poetry are present from the beginning of Verlaine's writing. After the *Poèmes saturniens,* his first collection, the mixture of both is a more distinctive division and interleaving of the two; *Fêtes galantes* is followed by *La Bonne Chanson, Romances sans paroles* by *Sagesse.* Thereafter, with the exception of occasional poems, his poetry generally follows the line of sentimentality established in *La Bonne Chanson.* Seemingly the more Verlaine sought moral responsibility in his life, be it through marriage to Mathilde, a return to Cathol-

icism, or teaching in England, the more his poetry resounds
with earnest sentimentality which easily bores:

> On sort de l'église, après les vêpres,
> Pour la procession si touchante
> Qui a nom: du vœu Louis Treize:
> C'est le cas de prier pour la France.
>
> (*Bonheur,* XXIX, 17-20)

The collection *Parallèlement* (1889) at least is less self-
deceiving in its portrayal of what Verlaine perceives as his
two natures, the saintly and the demonic, and which amounts
to a rudimentary and unhelpful division of himself into the
spiritual and the physical. Unlike Baudelaire, Verlaine is
singularly untroubled by the effort to unite the moral and the
feeling person, quite possibly even by the awareness of such a
need. Indeed responses to the merits of these collections vary
accordingly. Some will be moved by Verlaine's sincere wish
for salvation in marriage as in Catholicism, others will find it
embarrassing, outrageous even. *Fêtes galantes* and *Romances
sans paroles* invite a more straightforward response, for their
emotional tact and relative absence of self-persuading moralising make for a non-didactic kind of poetry. Nevertheless
many people do respond to Verlaine's longing for self-control
and so for 'happiness' as expressed in *La Bonne Chanson* and
Sagesse. Such poetry is a testimony to a distressed person's
search for a refuge from himself and is to be respected as
such. Even so, the distinctive Verlainian achievement lies in
the poetry of *Fêtes galantes* and *Romances sans paroles.*
Verlaine's lack of curiosity, his refusal to pursue a single
aesthetic purpose, in a sense, his laziness, have produced a
sensibility remarkably free from intellectual and moral restric-
tions. Paradoxically this sensibility as expressed in the two
collections is, mostly, a poetry of emotional discretion and
conviction, together with an extension of the scope of poetic
expression, which embraces more fully than hitherto the
direct emotional power of music. As with any artist who
instinctively understands the strengths and limitations of his

or her talent, the result, in these collections, is an art of undoubted originality.

Baudelaire, Mallarmé, Rimbaud, each contributed to French poetry a particular vision, a particular ideal pertaining to a transcendental reality. Verlaine's contribution is a subjective idealism which seriously puts the proposition that we can know only our own emotional states. Verlaine's 'révolte' too is a no less significant contribution to poetry than to our understanding of the human condition. In this search for an Ideal, *Fêtes galantes* and *Romances sans paroles* may be considered a form of Symbolist poetry. Verlaine, of course, disclaimed any such definition and amusingly referred to these poets as 'Cymbalistes'. And he continues to have the last word on the matter in his comment on himself, under the anagram of 'Pauvre Lélian' in *Les Poètes maudits*:

> Un poète n'était-il pas libre de tout faire pourvu que tout fût bel et bien fait, ou devait-il se cantonner dans un genre, sous prétexte d'unité? (*2*, p. 688)

Selective Bibliography

PRIMARY SOURCES

1. *Œuvres poétiques complètes*, ed. Y.-G. Le Dantec, nouvelle édition révisée et présentée par J. Borel (Paris, Gallimard, Bibliothèque de la Pléiade, 1962). The standard edition, with notes tending to the useful rather than the illuminating.
2. *Œuvres en prose complètes*, ed. J. Borel (Paris, Gallimard, Bibliothèque de la Pléiade, 1972). As above.
3. *Album Verlaine*, ed. P. Petitfils (Paris, Gallimard, Album de la Pléiade, 1981). Rich visual documentation, up to the standard of this series.
4. *Œuvres complètes*, introduction by O. Nadal, study and note by J. Borel, text and notes by H. Bouillane de Lacoste (Paris, Club du meilleur livre, 2 vols, 1959 and 1960). Much fuller and more interesting presentation of Verlaine's work. Infuriatingly, the pages of introduction are not paginated.
5. *Fêtes galantes, La Bonne Chanson, and Romances sans paroles*, ed. V. P. Underwood (Manchester, Manchester University Press, 1942, reprinted 1955). Brief and meticulous introduction, with emphasis more on dates than on interpretation.
6. *Romances sans paroles*, ed. D. Hillery (London, Athlone Press, 1976). Useful bibliography.
7. *Fêtes galantes, La Bonne Chanson, Romances sans paroles, Ecrits sur Rimbaud*, ed. J. Gaudon (Paris, Garnier-Flammarion, 1976). The recommended edition, both for the material on the Verlaine-Rimbaud relationship and for the reasonable price.
8. *Correspondance*, ed. A. van Bever (Paris, Messein, 3 vols, 1922-29; reprint Geneva, Slatkine, 1983).

SECONDARY SOURCES

9. A. Adam, *Verlaine* (Paris, Hatier, Connaissance des lettres, 1953, new edition 1965). Very good general study giving full account of both Verlaine and his work. Inclines to psychological interpretations of the poems.
10. C. Baudelaire, *Œuvres complètes*, ed. C. Pichois (Paris, Gallimard, Bibliothèque de la Pléiade, 2 vols, 1975 and 1976).

11. J.-H. Bornecque, _Lumières sur les 'Fêtes galantes' de Paul Verlaine_ (Paris, Nizet, 1969). Thorough and interesting. Again a bias to a psychological reading of the poems.

12. ———, 'L'Œil double et les motivations verlainiennes dans _Romances sans paroles_' in _La Petite Musique de Verlaine_ (Paris, Sedes, 1982, pp. 97-113). Interesting study of poems in perspective of 'double lecture' of life and art. Saved from the banal by stressing Verlaine's desire for, and fear of flight.

13. ———, 'Le Problème des _Fêtes galantes_' in _Mélanges offerts à Daniel Mornet_ (Paris, Nizet, 1951).

14. ———, _Verlaine par lui-même_ (Paris, Seuil, 1966). Rather overwritten and self-fulfilling, but sound enough and with interesting pictures.

15. A. Brookner, _Watteau_ (London, Hamlyn, 1967). Lucid study.

16. F.-A. Cazals and G. Le Rouge, _Les Derniers Jours de Paul Verlaine_ (Paris, Mercure de France, 1911). A good read, if you don't believe it all. Gives the flavour of the period, and has merit of being written (albeit greatly aided by Le Rouge) by a close friend of Verlaine's. See _20_ and _23_.

17. J. F. Chaussivert, 'Fête et jeu verlainiens', in _La Petite Musique de Verlaine_ (Paris, Sedes, 1982), pp. 49-60.

18. C. Cuénot, 'L'Evolution poétique de Paul Verlaine', in _Le Ruban rouge_ (Paris, no. 10, Sept. 1961), pp. 54-64. Thorough account, and particularly interesting on the _Romances_ as Verlaine's own 'new' poetry.

19. ———, _Le Style de Paul Verlaine_ (Paris, C.D.U., 1962). Major and seemingly inexhaustible study of Verlaine's stylistic procedures. Useful mainly as reference work.

20. E. Delahaye, _Verlaine_ (Paris, Messein, 1919). Also by a friend of Verlaine. See _16_ and _23_.

21. D. Hillery, _Music and Poetry in France from Baudelaire to Mallarmé_ (Bern, Peter Lang, 1980). Thoughtful study of connections between these arts as perceived by the artists themselves. Ultimately frustrating in its refusal to draw conclusions.

22. J. Huret, _Enquête sur l'évolution littéraire_ (Paris, Charpentier, 1891, nouvelle éditon, Paris, Thot, 1982). The source book on many nineteenth-century poets' views on 'l'évolution littéraire'. Eminently readable, and indeed funny in parts. Usually interesting.

23. E. Lepelletier, _Paul Verlaine: sa vie, son œuvre_ (Paris, Mercure de France, 1923). Not much on 'son œuvre'. Yet another biography by a friend of Verlaine. See _16_ and _20_.

24. S. Mallarmé, _Œuvres complètes,_ ed. H. Mondor and G. Jean-Aubry (Paris, Gallimard, Bibliothèque de la Pléiade, 1945).

25. P. Martino, _Verlaine_ (Paris, Boivin, 1924). Sensible study.

26. G. Michaud, _De la Musique avant toute chose_ (Saarbrücken, Universität des Saarlands, 1952, pp. 83-100). Very detailed study of the 'structures sonores' of three poems. Methodical, diagrammatic analysis, more than compensated for by sensible and sometimes illuminating conclusions drawn from these data.

27. D. J. Mossop, *The Origins of the Idea of 'Pure Poetry'* (Durham, University of Durham, 1964). Intricate, meticulous and readable study.

28. ———, *Pure Poetry*. *Studies in French poetic theory and practice, 1746-1945* (Oxford, Clarendon Press, 1971). Arguably the definitive study on this subject.

29. O. Nadal. See *4*. Nadal's introduction largely subsumes various articles. His *Paul Verlaine* (Paris, Mercure de France, 1961) is both sensitive and sensible. Valuable chapter on 'songe' and 'rêverie'.

30. ———, "Rêve d'action chez P. Verlaine', in *Mercure de France* (Paris, 1 December 1959), pp. 648-683.

31. P. Petitfils, *Verlaine* (Paris, Julliard, 1981). Fully documented and lively biography.

32. J.-P. Richard, 'Fadeur de Verlaine', in *Poésie et profondeur* (Paris, Seuil, 1955). Deep and thought-provoking study of degrees of 'disembodied' sensations. Style tends to the indirect.

33. J. Richardson, *Verlaine* (London, Weidenfeld and Nicolson, 1971). Well researched, but lacks vitality.

34. J. Richer, *Paul Verlaine* (Paris, Seghers, Poètes d'aujourd'hui, 1960). Excellent introduction, comprehensive and to the point.

35. A. Rimbaud, *Œuvres complètes,* ed. A. Adam (Paris, Gallimard, Bibliothèque de la Pléiade, 1972).

36. P. Soulié-Lapeyre, *Le Vague et l'aigu dans la perception verlainienne* (Paris, Les Belles Lettres, 1975). Very thorough, semi-psychoanalytic study, but the 'vague' - 'aigu' connexion invites consideration of 'Précis' and 'Indécis'.

37. P. Stephan, 'Verlaine's distant emotions', in *The Romanic Review* (vol. 52, no. 3, 1961), pp. 198-209. A study of Verlaine's 'distancing' from the emotions with interesting emphasis on humour, wit and irony. Pertinent.

38. V. P. Underwood, *Verlaine et l'Angleterre* (Paris, Nizet, 1956). Takes approach of comparative literature. Full documentation of Verlaine's stays in England. Not directly relevant to the present study.

39. *Watteau 1648-1721* (Paris, Editions de la Réunion des musées nationaux, 1984). Excellent coverage by experts of all relevant aspects of Watteau, his work, his period. Well-printed reproductions.

40. G. Zayed, *Formation littéraire de Verlaine* (Geneva, Droz, 1956). Demonstrates both Verlaine's receptivity to literary influence and the nature of his poetic originality. Good bibliography.

41. ———, 'Les *Romances sans paroles* ou la nostalgie du paradis perdu', in *L'Icosathèque (20th),* 2 (Paris, Minard, 1975). Argues that the *Romances* are 'about' Mathilde. I do not share his view, but I find many remarks insightful.

42. ———, 'Les Secrets des *Ariettes oubliées',* in *La Petite Musique de Verlaine* (Paris, Sedes, 1982), pp. 31-44. See my comments for *41*.

43. E. M. Zimmerman, *Magies de Verlaine, étude de l'évolution poétique de Paul Verlaine* (Paris, Corti, 1967). Thorough and worthwhile study of Verlaine's development of his 'poetic system'. Lengthy and subtle commentaries on the poems.

CRITICAL GUIDES TO FRENCH TEXTS

edited by

Roger Little, Wolfgang van Emden, David Williams

DATE DUE